I0827828

J. Chester

The Gay Divorcee's Survival Guide

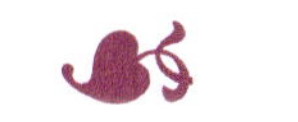

The Gay Divorcee's Survival Guide
002 Edition

FICTIONAL CHARACTERS NOTICE: The characters Marcus and Deja appearing in this book are entirely fictional composite characters created for illustrative purposes. They are not based on any single real individual, living or deceased. Any resemblance to actual persons, living or dead, or actual events is purely coincidental. No composite character in this book is intended to represent, depict, or identify any specific individual.

QUOTATION NOTICE: Quotations appearing in this book are attributed to their known or commonly cited sources and are used for commentary, criticism, and educational purposes consistent with the principles of fair use under 17 U.S.C. § 107. Where original authorship is uncertain or disputed, quotations are identified as "Unknown." The author makes no claim of ownership over quoted material.

DISCLAIMER: The information provided in this book is for general informational, educational, and entertainment purposes only. It is not intended as legal, professional, financial, or therapeutic advice, and should not be relied upon as such. The LGBTQ+-specific legal information contained herein reflects general awareness and is not a substitute for qualified legal counsel familiar with the laws of your specific jurisdiction. Laws vary significantly by state and country and are subject to change.

The author and publisher are not responsible for any actions taken based on the information presented in this book. Readers should consult with appropriately licensed attorneys, financial advisors, mental health professionals, and other qualified experts for advice tailored to their individual circumstances. The author and publisher make no representations or warranties regarding the accuracy, completeness, or reliability of the content herein. Any reliance on the information provided is solely at the reader's own risk. The author and publisher expressly disclaim any liability for any loss, injury, or damages of any kind incurred directly or indirectly from the use of, or reliance upon, this book.

PERSONAL NARRATIVE NOTICE: Portions of this book reflect the author's personal experiences and perspective. These personal reflections are the author's own and are not intended to characterize, identify, or make claims about any other individual. The author's personal story is shared solely for the purpose of connection and illustration, and no inference should be drawn regarding any third party.

For permissions, wholesale inquiries, or speaking engagements:
Jarvaris Chester ~ The Gilded Peacock ~ J's Personal Services LLC
jspersonalservicesllc@gmail.com

Hard Cover ISBN: 979-8-9884648-0-8
Paper Back ISBN: 979-8-9884648-2-2

Library of Congress Cataloging-in-Publication Data has been applied for.

THE GAY DIVORCEE'S SURVIVAL GUIDE

Second Edition 2026

by J. Chester

"Because you deserve more than just surviving."

Prologue

I Burned the Map. Then I Found My Way.

The first edition of this book saved my life. Not in a dramatic way but in a quiet, 2 a.m., sitting-on-the-bathroom-floor kind of way. Writing it forced me to make sense of something that felt completely senseless. And if even one person read it and felt less alone, then every word was worth it.

But here's the thing about growth: it shows you where you were standing before you moved. And when I looked back at that first edition, I saw a man who was still in the thick of it, trying to write his way through the smoke. What you're holding now is written from the other side of the fire. My name is JC. I was married for eight years. Eight years of building a life with someone ~ inside jokes, inside scars, shared passwords, shared dreams. And then one day, slowly and then all at once, it was over. The divorce didn't just end my marriage. It ended a version of me. And honestly? That version needed to go.

This second edition is not a patch job on the first. It's a rebuild. Because you deserve a guide written by someone who has not only been through the earthquake but has also done the unglamorous work of clearing the rubble ~ therapy, tears, awkward first dates, bad decisions, better decisions, chosen family dinners that became the highlight of my week, and mornings that finally started feeling like possibilities instead of problems.

This book is for everyone walking through divorce ~ regardless of who you loved, who left, who stayed, or who you're becoming. Because pain does not discriminate. Neither does healing.

You're going to meet two people throughout these pages. Marcus is a 41-year-old gay man navigating divorce after a 12-year marriage that looked perfect from the outside and felt suffocating from the inside. Deja is a 35-year-old bisexual woman untangling a marriage that started beautifully and ended in betrayal. Their stories are composite ~ inspired by real people, real situations, real pain ~ but their voices are entirely their own.

"If standing up for yourself means burning a bridge, I have a box of matches. We ride at Dawn." ~ Unknown

That quote opened the first edition. It still opens this one. Because some things don't change. But the way we carry them does.

Let's go.

~ JC

Chapter 1

The Earthquake
When Everything Falls Apart

Nobody tells you what the first day actually feels like.

They tell you divorce is hard. They tell you it takes time. They hand you casseroles and platitudes and the name of a good lawyer. But nobody sits you down and says: there will be a moment ~ maybe in your car, maybe in the cereal aisle, maybe at 3 a.m. staring at the ceiling ~ where your whole body will feel like it's been unplugged from the wall. Like the person you were before this moment has simply left the building.

That's the earthquake. And if you're reading this, you've probably already felt it.

Welcome, love. You are not broken. You are just in the rubble right now, and rubble is a place you can build from.

Meet Marcus

Marcus had a system for everything. Color-coded calendar. Standing Sunday meal prep. A five-year plan that had been revised so many times it barely resembled the original.

What Marcus did not have a system for was the Tuesday afternoon his husband of twelve years sat down across from him at their kitchen table and said the words Marcus had been quietly dreading for two years.

"I think we both know this isn't working anymore."

Marcus told me later that what surprised him most wasn't the sadness. He'd expected the sadness. What floored him was the relief ~ a small, shameful flicker of it ~ right underneath the grief. And then the guilt about the relief. And then the grief about the guilt. By Thursday he hadn't eaten a

real meal and was watching cooking competition shows at midnight just to hear other people's voices.
That's the earthquake. It doesn't always look like screaming. Sometimes it looks like silence.

Meet Deja

Deja found out on a Wednesday. She'd been suspicious for months ~ the late nights, the locked phone, the way her husband said her name differently, like it had become a task instead of a word he loved.
When she confirmed what she already knew, she didn't cry. Not at first. She packed a bag, drove to her best friend's apartment, sat on the couch, and stared at the wall for four hours. Her friend ordered Thai food. They watched terrible reality TV. Nobody said anything particularly useful.
But Deja told me something I haven't forgotten: "The worst part wasn't finding out. The worst part was realizing I'd already known. And I'd been lying to myself just as much as he'd been lying to me."
That kind of honesty? That's where healing actually starts. Not in the moment you find out. In the moment you stop pretending.

What the First Days Actually Feel Like

Let's skip the clinical list of grief stages for a second and just be real. The first days of a divorce ~ whether it was your decision, their decision, or a mutual slow collapse ~ tend to feel something like this:
One moment you're fine. Actually fine. You feel clear and strong and like you have finally made the right choice or finally accepted the inevitable.
The next moment you're on the bathroom floor.
Both of those moments are valid. Both of those moments are part of the process. The earthquake doesn't happen once ~ it has aftershocks. Some days will feel like you've moved ten steps forward. Other days you'll wake up and the grief will be sitting right on your chest like it never left.

Here's what I want you to know: that is not failure. That is not weakness. That is what it looks like to be a human being losing something that mattered.

"Grief is just love with nowhere to go." ~ Jamie Anderson

You loved this person. Maybe you still do. Maybe you love the version of them you thought they were, or the version of your life you thought you'd have. All of that is real. All of that deserves to be grieved. Don't let anyone ~ including yourself ~ rush you past it.

The Emotional Reality Nobody Talks About

Here's what the pamphlets leave out: divorce grief is not linear. It does not move from denial to acceptance in a tidy arc. It loops. It doubles back. It hides for two weeks and then ambushes you at a wedding.

You might feel relief and then feel guilty about the relief. You might feel grief and then feel angry at yourself for grieving someone who hurt you. You might feel completely numb for a month and then sob at a song you don't even like.

All of it is normal. All of it is part of the same process.

What helps is not pretending the feelings aren't there. What helps is letting them move through you without letting them make all your decisions.

Marcus learned to give himself a 20-minute window each evening to feel whatever he needed to feel ~ fully, without judgment ~ and then close it. Like a tab he'd return to but didn't need open all day. It sounds clinical. It worked.

Deja journaled. Not because she's a journaling person ~ she'll tell you she's absolutely not a journaling person ~ but because she needed somewhere to put thoughts that were too jagged to say out loud. The pages didn't judge her. They just held it.

You'll find your version of this. The point is to find something that lets the feelings out without letting them run the show.

The First 30 Days ~ Your Emotional First Aid Kit

Before we get into the legal, financial, and logistical reality of divorce ~ which we absolutely will, in detail ~ I want to give you some grounding for the immediate aftermath. Because none of the practical stuff is navigable if you're in complete free-fall.

One: let yourself not be okay. This is not the time to perform strength. It is okay to tell the people who love you that you are not fine. You do not have to hold it together all the time. Strength is not the absence of falling apart ~ it's what you do when you get back up.

Two: eat something. Drink water. Sleep when you can. This sounds embarrassingly basic but grief lives in the body, and your body needs fuel to carry it. You cannot process emotions on an empty stomach and four hours of sleep indefinitely.

Three: identify your one safe person. Not ten people. One. The person you can call at midnight who will not give you advice, will not take sides, will not make it about themselves. Just sits with you. If you don't have that person yet, this book will help you build that.

Four: stay off their social media. I shouldn't have to say this but I'm going to say it anyway: nothing good lives there right now. Nothing. Close the app. Block if you need to. Protect your healing like it's the most important thing you own ~ because it is.

Five: don't make any major decisions for the first 30 days if you can help it. Not about where to live, not about who to date, not about what to say publicly, not about whether to fight for the house. Your nervous system is in survival mode. Let it stabilize before you start making calls you'll have to live with.

A Note on LGBTQ+ Divorce ~ The Weight Others Don't Carry

For many of us in the LGBTQ+ community, divorce carries a weight that straight divorcees simply don't have to reckon with.

We fought ~ legally, socially, sometimes within our own families ~ for the right to get married in the first place. For some of us, that marriage was a profound act of visibility and defiance. And now, when it ends, there's a complicated grief that's not just about the relationship. It's about what the relationship represented.

There may be family members who say "I told you so" in ways that are thinly veiled as concern. There may be community members who treat your divorce as evidence of something ~ about your identity, your choices, your worth. There may be an internal voice that asks whether you fought for something you didn't deserve.

Let me be clear: you deserved every right you fought for. Marriages end. Straight ones end too ~ at roughly the same rate, if you'd like the receipts. Your divorce is not a referendum on your identity or your community. It is the end of one relationship. That's all.

Marcus told me the hardest conversation he had wasn't with his ex. It was with his mother, who had finally come around to accepting his marriage and who took the divorce as a kind of personal loss of the son-in-law she'd grown to love. Grief is complicated. Love is complicated. None of that is your fault to fix.

Deja's experience was different ~ she faced questions from people who had never fully accepted that her bisexuality was "real," and who used her divorce to reignite those doubts. She learned to stop explaining herself to people who had already decided what they believed. That too is a form of healing.

We'll return to these themes throughout the book ~ in the legal chapter, in co-parenting, in dating again. But for now, just know: whatever extra weight you're carrying, I see it. And this book was written with it in mind.

You Are Not Starting Over. You Are Starting From.

There's a phrase people love to say to someone going through divorce: "You're starting over."

I'd like to gently retire that phrase.

Starting over implies that everything before this moment was erased ~ was wasted, was a mistake. And that's not true. You are not starting over. You are starting from. From everything you learned. From every way this relationship shaped you, challenged you, broke you open. From the version of yourself that survived it.

That is not zero. That is an enormous amount.

Marcus started from 41 years of knowing himself well enough to finally admit what wasn't working. Deja started from the clarity that comes when you stop lying to yourself.

You are starting from wherever you are. And wherever that is ~ it's enough.

Let's build from here.

Chapter 2

Is This Really It? Deciding With Clarity

Before we go any further, I need to say something out loud. This chapter is not here to talk you into divorce. It is not here to talk you out of it either. It is here to help you get honest ~ radically, uncomfortably, lovingly honest ~ with yourself about what you actually want, what is actually happening, and what you are actually capable of living with.
Because the decision to end a marriage is one of the most significant choices a human being can make. It deserves more than a bad week. It deserves more than a gut feeling. And it also deserves more than years of quiet suffering because you were too afraid to admit that something was fundamentally broken.

So let's sit in this together. No rushing.

The Question Underneath the Question

Most people who are considering divorce aren't actually asking "should I get divorced?" What they're really asking is something closer to: Is it okay to want more than this? Am I allowed to leave? Did I try hard enough? Will I regret this? Am I the problem?
Those are the real questions. And they deserve real answers.
Marcus spent two years asking himself whether he was just being selfish. His marriage wasn't abusive. His husband wasn't a bad person. They had a beautiful home, a shared friend group, a life that looked like the kind of life you were supposed to want. But behind closed doors, Marcus felt invisible. Not maltreated ~ invisible. Like he had become furniture in his own life. Functional. Unnoticed.

He kept telling himself that invisible wasn't a good enough reason to blow up a twelve-year marriage. He kept waiting for something dramatic to happen so he'd have permission.

Here's what I told Marcus, and what I'll tell you: invisible is a reason. Chronically unseen and unheard in your own partnership is a reason. You do not need a dramatic inciting incident to justify the quiet erosion of your soul.

Deja's situation looked different on the surface ~ the infidelity gave her a clear, undeniable reason. But even she found herself second-guessing it. Maybe she'd been too distant. Maybe she'd pushed him away. Maybe if she just worked harder on herself~

Stop. Let me say this clearly: being betrayed is not a symptom of your inadequacy. It is a choice someone else made. Full stop.

Whatever brought you to this chapter, your reasons are valid. But clarity ~ real clarity ~ means understanding those reasons fully, not just feeling them.

Why People Choose Divorce ~ The Honest Version

The first edition of this book gave you a list of reasons. This edition gives you the truth underneath the list.

Infidelity is one of the most common reasons people file for divorce, and also one of the most complicated to navigate emotionally. The betrayal is real. The damage to trust is real. But what makes infidelity so particularly devastating is not just the act ~ it's the realization that your partner was capable of building a secret life while sharing a real one with you. That's a specific kind of grief. It doesn't just hurt your heart. It scrambles your sense of reality.

Rebuilding after infidelity is possible. Couples do it. But it requires the unfaithful partner to do sustained, unglamorous work ~ not just apologies, but accountability. Therapy. Transparency. Time. And it requires the betrayed partner to genuinely want to rebuild, not just fear what leaving looks like. If either of those pieces is missing, the relationship will limp forward until it collapses under the weight of unresolved damage.

Deja: *"I gave us six months in couples therapy after I found out. I wanted to want to stay. But every time I looked at him, I was doing math in my head ~ calculating how long it had been going on, wondering what I missed, resenting that I had to work this hard on something he broke. That's when I knew. I didn't want to rebuild this. I wanted to be free of it."*

Growing apart is less dramatic but just as real. People change. Interests shift. The person you married at 27 may have almost nothing in common with who you are at 42 ~ and neither of you did anything wrong. The tragedy of growing apart is that there's no villain. Just two people who loved each other and then slowly, quietly, became strangers living in the same house.

Irreconcilable differences ~ values, life goals, fundamental worldviews ~ can erode a marriage the way water erodes stone. Slowly, invisibly, until one day you realize the foundation is gone. If one partner wants children and the other doesn't. If one partner's faith has deepened and the other has walked away from it entirely. If one partner wants roots and the other wants to run. These aren't failures of love. They're mismatches of direction.

Financial conflict is one of the leading causes of divorce, and it's rarely actually about money. It's about values, power, security, trust, and control. The partner who hides purchases is hiding something about themselves. The partner who controls all the finances is controlling more than money. When two people cannot find a shared language for how they handle resources, they often cannot find a shared language for how they build a life.

Substance abuse and addiction create a particular kind of grief in a marriage ~ because you often end up mourning someone who is still physically present. The person you fell in love with is still there, somewhere underneath the addiction. And that makes leaving feel like abandonment even when it is survival. If this is your situation, I want to say this gently and clearly: loving someone with an addiction does not obligate you to sacrifice your own well-being. You can love someone and still choose to leave.

Abuse ~ physical, emotional, psychological, financial ~ is never a gray area. It is never a reason to stay and work harder. It is a reason to leave, and to do so safely, with support, with a plan. If this is your situation, please turn to the resources section at the back of this book before anything else.

The Pros and Cons ~ But Make Them Real

Everyone tells you to make a pros and cons list. Fine. But most people make a pros and cons list of the divorce itself ~ the logistics, the practicalities, the fear. That's not the list you need.

The list you need is this: What does staying cost me? And what does leaving cost me?

Not financially. Not yet. Emotionally. Energetically. In terms of who you are becoming and who you want to be.

Staying in a marriage that is no longer working costs you something every single day. It costs you the quiet erosion of your self-worth when you feel unseen. It costs you the slow dimming of your joy when you stop expecting things to get better. It costs you the version of yourself you could be becoming if you weren't spending all your energy managing a broken dynamic.

Leaving costs you something too. The grief of the ending. The upheaval of a life restructured. The fear of the unknown. The real and significant pain of disentangling two lives that were built together. If children are involved, the complexity multiplies.

Neither of those lists cancels the other out. But writing them out ~ honestly, without performing either martyrdom or bravado ~ gives you something to actually reckon with instead of a fog of anxiety and indecision.

Marcus: *"I made the list three times over two years. The first two times I talked myself out of it. The third time I looked at the 'cost of staying' column and realized I'd* *stopped adding anything to the 'reason to stay' column. It was just blank. And that blank space was more honest than anything I'd said out loud."*

A Note for LGBTQ+ Readers ~ The Pressures Others Don't Feel

If you exist in the LGBTQ+ community and are considering divorce, there are pressures on your decision that most mainstream divorce guides don't acknowledge. Let's name them.

The visibility burden. For many of us, our marriage was a public act. It was seen by our families, our communities, our workplaces as a statement ~ proof of our legitimacy, our normalcy, our right to the same things straight people take for granted. When that marriage ends, some people will treat it as proof of something negative. About you. About queer relationships in general. About whether we deserved the rights we fought for.

Let me be unambiguous: your marriage ending does not mean queer love doesn't work. Straight marriages end every day and nobody uses them to question the validity of heterosexuality. Your divorce is not a data point in anyone's argument. It is a private human experience, and it belongs to you.

The community judgment factor. LGBTQ+ communities can be extraordinarily supportive ~ and they can also be extraordinarily small and interconnected. If you and your partner share a friend group, a community space, a chosen family network, the social fallout of divorce can feel uniquely suffocating. You may worry about losing not just your partner but your entire world.

This is a real concern and we'll address it in depth in the chapters on chosen family and community rebuilding. For now, know this: the people who are truly your people will not make you choose. And the ones who do make you choose have already told you something important about themselves.

The coming out again reality. For some LGBTQ+ people, particularly those who came out later in life or whose marriage was part of their coming out journey, divorce means another kind of coming out. Coming out as someone who tried and didn't make it. Coming out to family members who may have just gotten comfortable. Coming out to yourself as someone whose story is still being written.

That is exhausting. It is also brave. And it is survivable.

The legal complexity. In many states and countries, LGBTQ+ marriages ~ particularly those that predate marriage equality ~ exist in complicated legal territory. Parental rights for non-biological parents, asset division when marriages weren't legally recognized for their full duration, and inconsistent state-by-state protections all add layers to an already complex process. We will cover this in full in Chapter 3. Go in informed.

The Alternatives ~ When Divorce Isn't the Only Door

Before we talk about how to leave, let's talk about whether leaving is what you actually need. Because sometimes what looks like a dying marriage is a marriage in crisis ~ and those are different things.

Couples therapy, done well, with a therapist who specializes in relationships and whom both partners are genuinely committed to, can be transformative. Not as a last resort after years of damage, but as a real investment in figuring out what's actually broken and whether it can be repaired.

The key word is genuinely. One partner dragging the other to therapy while the other mentally checks out is not couples therapy. It's a very expensive performance.

A trial separation is not giving up. It is sometimes the only way to get enough distance to see the relationship clearly. When you are inside something every single day, you lose perspective. A structured separation ~ with clear terms, a set timeline, individual therapy for each partner, and defined expectations ~ can reveal whether you miss each other or whether you feel relief. Both of those answers are information.

Mediation, before things get adversarial, can also be a way of deciding together rather than through lawyers and litigation. If both partners are still capable of sitting in a room and having a productive conversation, a skilled mediator can help you figure out whether there's a path forward ~ or help you design a respectful exit if there isn't.

Collaborative divorce is worth knowing about. It involves both partners working with a team of professionals ~ attorneys, financial specialists, sometimes mental health professionals ~ to reach a settlement without going to court. It is typically less expensive, less traumatic, and faster than litigation. We'll cover it more in Chapter 3.

None of these alternatives mean you have to stay. They mean you have options worth considering before you decide. And if you've already tried some or all of them ~ if you've done the therapy, attempted the conversations, sat in the silence ~ then you already have your answer. And that answer is enough.

How to Know When You Know

People ask me all the time: how did you know it was really over? And I always say the same thing.

I knew when I stopped hoping it would get better and started hoping it would just end.

There is a difference between the grief of a relationship going through a hard season and the grief of a relationship that has run its course. Hard seasons feel like something you want to fight through. Endings feel like something you are waiting to be released from.

You may have already felt that shift. That moment when you stopped imagining a future with this person and started imagining a future without them ~ and the future without them felt like oxygen.

Or you may still be in the fog, unsure whether what you're feeling is clarity or fear wearing clarity's mask. That's okay too. That's what this book is for.

"The most difficult thing is the decision to act. The rest is merely tenacity." ~ Amelia Earhart

Whatever you decide ~ to stay and fight for it, to leave and build something new, or to sit in the uncertainty a little longer ~ make the decision consciously. Make it eyes open. Make it from a place of honesty with yourself rather than from panic, inertia, or what you think you're supposed to do. You are the only one who has to live inside your choice. Make it count.

Chapter 3

Lawyer Up
Navigating the Legal Maze

Let me tell you what nobody told me before I hired my first divorce attorney.

Your lawyer is not your therapist. Your lawyer is not your friend. Your lawyer is not your revenge machine. Your lawyer is a skilled professional whose job is to protect your legal interests and navigate a system that was not designed with your emotional well-being in mind. The sooner you understand that distinction, the better ~ both for your sanity and for your bank account.

Because every phone call, every email, every tearful voicemail you leave at 11 p.m. is being billed. Every time you ask your attorney to read a text your ex sent you about the dog, you are paying for that. Every meeting that drifts from legal strategy into venting is costing you money you could use to rebuild your life.

I say this not to make you feel bad but to make you prepared. Because when you're prepared, you're powerful. And in a legal process that can feel completely out of your control, information is the closest thing to power you're going to get. So let's get you powerful.

Before You Call Anyone ~ What to Do First

Before you hire an attorney, before you serve papers, before you say a single word to your spouse about your legal intentions, there are things you need to do quietly and quickly.

Gather your financial documents. Bank statements, tax returns for the last three to five years, mortgage documents, retirement account statements, investment portfolios, credit card statements, car titles, business records if applicable. Make copies. Store them somewhere your spouse cannot access ~ a trusted friend's home, a safety deposit box in your name only, a secure cloud account they don't know about.

Document everything. If there has been any abuse, infidelity, financial misconduct, or behavior that may be relevant to your case, document it now. Screenshots, records, dates, witnesses. Not to be vindictive ~ to be protected. Evidence that exists before proceedings begin is far more credible than evidence that appears after.

Open an individual bank account if you don't already have one. You are going to need access to funds that are solely yours to cover legal fees, living expenses, and the logistical costs of separating a life. Do this quietly and legally ~ do not drain joint accounts, which can be used against you. Simply establish your own foothold.

Know what you have and what you owe. Make a complete inventory of all marital assets and all marital debts. Property, vehicles, savings, retirement accounts, credit card balances, loans, mortgages. You cannot protect what you don't know you have, and you cannot negotiate what you don't understand.

Marcus: *"I spent two weeks before I contacted an attorney just gathering paper. Statements, documents, anything financial I could put my hands on. My attorney later told me it was one of the most prepared she'd ever seen a client come in. It saved me hours of billable time and gave me leverage I didn't even know I had."*

Finding the Right Attorney ~ Not Just Any Attorney

Divorce attorneys are not interchangeable. The attorney who handled your neighbor's amicable separation is not necessarily the right person for your contested custody battle. The aggressive litigator who wins in court may be entirely wrong for a collaborative divorce. The fit matters enormously ~ for your outcome, your experience, and your wallet.

Start with referrals, but vet them independently. Ask people you trust who have been through divorce, ask your therapist or financial advisor if they work with clients in transition, check state bar association directories, look at reviews with a critical eye. A good referral is a starting point, not a final answer.

Look for specialization. Family law is its own world. You want someone whose practice is focused there, not a general attorney who handles divorces among a dozen other things. Within family law, consider whether your situation requires additional specialization ~ high-asset divorce, custody disputes, domestic violence, or LGBTQ+-specific expertise.

Interview at least three attorneys before you choose. Most offer initial consultations, some free and some for a fee. Use them. Ask about their experience with cases like yours, their approach to negotiation versus litigation, their communication style, their fee structure. Notice how they listen. Notice whether they make you feel heard or whether they're already calculating their strategy before you've finished your sentence.

Ask the hard money questions upfront. What is your retainer? What is your hourly rate? What is your rate for associates or paralegals who may work on my case? What are typical costs for a case like mine? How do you prefer to communicate and how quickly do you respond? These are not rude questions. These are necessary questions, and any attorney worth hiring will answer them directly.

Red flag: An attorney who promises you outcomes. No ethical attorney can guarantee results. What they can guarantee is competent, diligent representation.

Red flag: An attorney who encourages you to be adversarial when your situation doesn't require it. Litigation is expensive. Sometimes it's necessary. But an attorney who defaults to war when collaboration is possible is billing you for a war you didn't need to fight.

Red flag: An attorney who doesn't return calls or emails within a reasonable time. Communication in legal proceedings is everything. If they're slow before you're a client, imagine after.

Understanding How You'll Pay ~ And Making It Count

Most divorce attorneys work on retainer ~ you pay a lump sum upfront, and they draw their fees from that sum as they work on your case. When the retainer runs low, you replenish it. This is the most common arrangement, and it has one critical implication: every interaction costs money. This means your job is to be the most efficient client your attorney has ever worked with. Come to every meeting prepared. Bring organized documents, written questions, clear priorities. Send concise emails, not emotional monologues. Save the emotional processing for your therapist, your journal, your best friend, your chosen family ~ not your lawyer.

Before every communication with your attorney, ask yourself: is this a legal question or an emotional one? Legal questions go to your lawyer. Emotional ones go elsewhere. That discipline alone can save you thousands of dollars.

Keep a running document of questions between attorney communications so you can address multiple items in a single call rather than five separate ones. Organize your documents so you can find things quickly ~ your attorney's time is money, and so is the time their paralegal spends waiting for you to locate a bank statement.

Understand what flat-fee versus hourly means for your specific situation. Some attorneys offer flat fees for uncontested divorces. If your divorce is relatively straightforward and you and your spouse are in agreement on the major issues, this can be significantly more cost-effective. Ask whether this is an option.

Deja: *"I made a rule for myself. Before I contacted my attorney about anything, I had to write it down first. If I could figure it out myself or if it wasn't actually a legal question, I didn't send it. I probably saved myself three or four thousand dollars just by pausing before I hit send. Anger is expensive."*

Understanding the Legal Process ~ What Actually Happens

Divorce proceedings vary by state, but the general arc looks something like this ~ and knowing it in advance takes away some of its power to destabilize you.

Filing. One spouse files a petition for divorce with the court, which formally initiates proceedings. The other spouse is served with the papers and has a window of time to respond. If you are the one being served, do not panic and do not sign anything without consulting an attorney first.

Temporary orders. In many cases, especially those involving children, shared property, or financial support, the court may issue temporary orders that govern how things are handled while the divorce is pending. Who lives in the house. Who pays which bills. What the custody arrangement looks like in the interim. These are temporary but they set a tone ~ which is why having good legal representation from the very beginning matters.

Discovery. Both parties are required to disclose their financial information fully and honestly. This is not optional, and hiding assets during discovery is not just unethical ~ it is illegal and can have serious consequences if discovered. Your attorney will guide you through this process, which typically involves exchanging financial statements, bank records, tax returns, and sometimes depositions.

Negotiation and settlement. The vast majority of divorces ~ somewhere north of ninety percent ~ are settled without going to trial. This happens through negotiation between attorneys, through mediation, or through collaborative divorce processes. Settlement is almost always preferable to trial: it is faster, less expensive, and gives both parties more control over the outcome.

Trial. If negotiation fails, the case goes before a judge who makes the final decisions on property division, support, and custody. Trials are expensive, emotionally exhausting, and unpredictable. A judge who does not know you or your family is making decisions about your life. Avoid trial if at all possible ~ but know that your attorney will prepare you for it if necessary.

Final decree. Once all issues are resolved ~ either through settlement or trial ~ the court issues a final divorce decree. This is the legal end of your marriage. Keep this document. You will need it.

One more thing: educate yourself on the laws specific to your state. Divorce law varies significantly. Community property states divide marital assets equally. Equitable distribution states divide them fairly, which does not always mean equally. Residency requirements, waiting periods, grounds for divorce ~ these all differ. Your attorney will guide you, but going in with basic knowledge means you ask better questions and make more informed decisions.

Division of Property ~ What's Yours, What's Theirs, What's Both

Property division is where divorces often get the most contentious, because property is concrete in a way that feelings aren't. You can argue about who checked out of the marriage first forever. You cannot argue about who is listed on the deed.

Marital property is generally defined as anything acquired during the marriage, regardless of whose name it's in. The house you bought together. The retirement account in your name that grew during your years of marriage. The car, the furniture, the investment portfolio, the business you built. All of it is typically on the table.

Separate property is generally defined as anything you owned before the marriage, or anything you received during the marriage as a gift or inheritance specifically to you. This can get complicated ~ if you inherited money and deposited it into a joint account, it may have become marital property. If you owned a house before the marriage and your spouse contributed to the mortgage, they may have a claim. These nuances are exactly why you need an attorney.

Valuation matters enormously. You cannot divide what you haven't accurately valued. This may mean getting appraisals on real estate, having a business valued by a forensic accountant, or determining the current value of retirement accounts and pension plans. Skipping this step to save money on the front end almost always costs more on the back end.

Debt is divided too. The credit card debt accumulated during your marriage, the car loan, the home equity line of credit ~ these don't disappear in a divorce. They get assigned. Make sure you understand who is responsible for what and ~ critically ~ ensure that any debt assigned to your spouse is actually transferred out of your name. A divorce decree says your ex is responsible for a credit card. The credit card company doesn't care about your divorce decree. If your name is on the account and payments stop, your credit takes the hit.

Marcus: *"Nobody told me about the debt thing until it was almost too late. My attorney caught it. We had a joint credit card that was assigned to my ex in the settlement, but it took three months to get my name actually removed from the account. In that window, I was still legally liable. Read everything. Ask about everything."*

Custody and Support ~ When Children Are Involved

If you have children, custody and support are where the legal process becomes the most emotional ~ and where clear heads matter most. Because every decision you make here will shape your children's daily lives for years.

There are two types of custody. Legal custody refers to the right to make major decisions about your child's life ~ medical care, education, religious upbringing. Physical custody refers to where the child lives day to day. Both can be sole or shared, and the arrangements for each are determined independently.

Courts determine custody based on one standard and one standard only: the best interest of the child. Not the punishment of either parent. Not the rewarding of the more sympathetic party. The child's well-being. Factors considered typically include each parent's relationship with the child, the stability of each home environment, each parent's willingness to support the child's relationship with the other parent, the child's own preferences depending on age, and any history of abuse or neglect.

Child support is calculated based on a formula that varies by state, typically taking into account each parent's income, the number of children, the custody arrangement, and certain expenses like childcare and healthcare. It is not a punishment and it is not a reward ~ it is a financial structure designed to ensure children are adequately supported by both parents regardless of which household they're in.

Spousal support, also called alimony, may be awarded based on factors including the length of the marriage, each partner's earning capacity, contributions made to the household including non-financial contributions like caregiving, and the standard of living established during the marriage. It is not guaranteed and it is not permanent in most cases. Know what the standards are in your state.

Modification is possible. Custody arrangements and support orders can be modified when there is a significant change in circumstances ~ a job loss, a relocation, a change in the child's needs. Build flexibility into your agreements and document everything, because life changes and the legal structures around your children may need to change with it.

LGBTQ+-Specific Legal Considerations ~ What You Need to Know

This section matters. Please read it carefully even if you think it doesn't apply to you, because some of these issues have a way of surfacing when you least expect them.

Marriage equality is federal law in the United States as of 2015, which means same-sex marriages are legally recognized in all fifty states. However, the legal landscape for LGBTQ+ divorce is still evolving and is not always as straightforward as it should be. Here's what to know.

Pre-equality relationships and asset division. If you and your partner were together for many years before you could legally marry ~ which is true for countless LGBTQ+ couples ~ the legal marriage date and the actual relationship start date may be very different. In many states, the division of assets is calculated based on the length of the legal marriage, not the relationship. This means years of shared financial contributions, shared property, and shared lives may not be recognized in the division. An attorney with LGBTQ+ family law experience will know how to argue for the broader picture.

Non-biological parental rights. This is one of the most urgent and emotionally charged legal issues in LGBTQ+ divorce. If one partner is the biological parent and the other is not ~ and if the non-biological parent did not complete a second-parent adoption or establish legal parentage through other means ~ the non-biological parent may have limited or no legal rights to the child, regardless of how involved they were in raising them. If this is your situation, consult an LGBTQ+-specialized family law attorney immediately. Do not wait. The time to establish legal parentage is before a divorce proceeding, not during one.

Interstate complications. LGBTQ+ legal protections are not uniform across all states. If you or your spouse lives in or relocates to a state with less protective laws, or if your divorce involves assets or property in multiple states, the legal complexity multiplies. Your attorney should be aware of and proactive about these cross-jurisdictional issues.

Discrimination in the process. While legal discrimination in divorce proceedings is prohibited, bias can still appear ~ in how judges rule on custody when one parent's sexual orientation is raised, in how attorneys approach your case, in how evaluators assess your fitness as a parent. Know your rights. Document any instance of apparent bias. And choose an attorney who will advocate for you aggressively if it happens.

Estate planning and beneficiary updates. The moment you decide to divorce, update your estate documents. Will, healthcare proxy, power of attorney, life insurance beneficiaries, retirement account beneficiaries. Your spouse may still be listed as the beneficiary on accounts that do not automatically update with a divorce decree. This is not a detail ~ this is your future.

Marcus: *"My attorney found out my ex was still listed as the beneficiary on a life insurance policy from before we were even legally married. We'd been together ten years before marriage equality passed. None of that showed up in the legal marriage record. If she hadn't caught it, he could have inherited that policy. Always check your beneficiaries. All of them."*

Alternatives to Traditional Litigation ~ Know Your Options

Litigation ~ going to court ~ is the most expensive, most time-consuming, and often most damaging way to get divorced. It should be a last resort, not a default. Here are the alternatives worth understanding.

Mediation involves a neutral third party ~ the mediator ~ who helps both spouses reach agreement on the issues in their divorce. The mediator does not take sides and does not make decisions. They facilitate conversation, help identify options, and guide the parties toward resolution. Mediation is typically faster and significantly less expensive than litigation. It works best when both parties are willing to engage in good faith and when the power dynamic between them is reasonably balanced.

Collaborative divorce takes mediation further. Both spouses have their own attorneys, and everyone agrees in advance to resolve the divorce without going to court. The team may also include financial specialists and mental health professionals. If the collaboration breaks down and the case goes to court, both attorneys are disqualified ~ which creates a strong incentive for everyone to stay at the table. It is one of the most humane ways to end a marriage.

Uncontested divorce is the simplest and least expensive option ~ it applies when both spouses agree on all major issues and simply need the court to formalize the agreement. Even in an uncontested divorce, having an attorney review the final agreement before you sign is worth every penny. What seems like a fair agreement in good faith can have long-term financial or legal consequences you don't see coming.

Online divorce services exist and work for some people in genuinely simple, fully uncontested situations with no children and minimal assets. If your situation is more complex than that ~ and most are ~ these services are not equipped to protect you. Use them with caution and always have an attorney review anything before it's filed.

Protecting Yourself ~ The Things People Forget

There are a handful of things people routinely forget in the legal process of divorce that come back to haunt them. Consider this your reminder.

Change your passwords. Every single one. Email, banking, social media, shared subscriptions, cloud storage, your phone's backup accounts. If your spouse knows your passwords ~ and after years of marriage they likely know at least some of them ~ change them now. Quietly and completely.

Remove your spouse from financial accounts where appropriate. Check with your attorney before doing anything with joint accounts ~ there are rules about what you can and cannot do with marital assets during proceedings. But establish individual accounts and begin moving your direct deposits and personal finances there.

Update your estate documents. As mentioned above ~ will, healthcare proxy, power of attorney, beneficiaries on all accounts and policies. Do not wait for the divorce to be final.

Be careful what you put in writing. Text messages, emails, social media posts ~ all of it can be used in legal proceedings. Do not text your ex things you would not want a judge to read. Do not post things on social media during your divorce that you would be embarrassed to have shown in court. And yes, people do subpoena social media.

Keep a record. Dates, times, conversations, incidents. Especially if custody or abuse is involved. Not obsessively ~

but consistently. A simple note in your phone with the date and a brief description of what happened is often enough. Courts respond to documentation.

Take care of your credit. Open accounts in your own name, begin building your individual credit history, and monitor your credit report regularly. Divorce can be a period of financial vulnerability. A strong credit foundation is protection.

"Knowledge is the antidote to fear." ~ Ralph Waldo Emerson

The legal process is designed for people who understand it. Now you understand it a little better. Use that.

Go in prepared. Go in clear-eyed. Go in with an attorney who fights for you and a support system that holds you. And know that the legal chapter of your divorce ~ as overwhelming as it feels right now ~ is temporary. It ends. And what comes after is yours to build.

Chapter 4

Show Me the Money
Financial Survival & Planning

Money is one of the last things people want to talk about when their heart is breaking. And I get it. When you are grieving the end of a marriage, balancing a budget feels impossibly small and impossibly heavy at the same time. But here is the truth that nobody leads with: financial clarity is one of the most powerful tools you have for reclaiming your life after divorce. Not because money is everything ~ it isn't. But because financial instability is one of the primary reasons people feel stuck after divorce. Fear of the numbers keeps people in situations they should have left sooner. Ignorance of the numbers leaves people blindsided by consequences they didn't see coming. And shame about the numbers ~ the debt, the dependency, the mess ~ keeps people from asking for the help they need.

This chapter is about all of it. The practical steps, yes. But also the emotional landscape of rebuilding financially ~ the fear, the shame, the anger, the slow and deeply satisfying work of building something that is entirely and unmistakably yours.

Let's open the books.

The Financial Reality Check ~ No Sugarcoating

Before you can build a financial future, you have to see your financial present clearly. Not the version you've been telling yourself, not the version that's easier to believe ~ the real version, with all its complications and embarrassments and surprises.

This means sitting down with every financial document you can get your hands on and building a complete picture. Every asset. Every liability. Every income stream. Every expense.

Every account in your name, every account in both names, every account you may not even know about.

Start with your assets. Bank accounts ~ checking, savings, money market ~ with current balances. Retirement accounts ~ 401(k), IRA, pension plans ~ with current values. Investment and brokerage accounts. Real estate, with current market values if possible. Vehicles, with current values. Business interests if applicable. Personal property of significant value ~ jewelry, art, collectibles. Life insurance policies with cash value.

Now the liabilities. Mortgage balance and monthly payment. Car loans. Credit card balances on every card ~ including cards you rarely use and may have forgotten about. Student loans. Personal loans. Medical debt. Any other outstanding obligations. Know the balance, the interest rate, and the minimum payment on every single one.

Then your income. Your salary or wages. Any bonuses, commissions, or variable income. Rental income if applicable. Investment income. Side income of any kind. And critically ~ income you may have been dependent on that is going away. If you've been living on a two-income household and you're about to become a one-income household, you need to see that gap clearly before it ambushes you.

And your monthly expenses. Housing ~ rent or mortgage, utilities, insurance, maintenance. Transportation ~ car payment, insurance, gas, public transit. Food ~ groceries and dining. Healthcare ~ insurance premiums, copays, prescriptions. Childcare if applicable. Debt payments. Subscriptions, memberships, recurring charges. Personal care. Entertainment. Clothing. Everything.

Write it all down. All of it. The number at the bottom of that exercise ~ the real number, the gap between what comes in and what goes out ~ is your starting point. It might be uncomfortable. It might be terrifying. It is also the most honest and useful thing you can know right now.

Deja: *"I had been managing the household finances for years and I thought I knew what we had. When I actually sat down and listed everything out for the first time as a* *single person, I found two credit cards I'd forgotten existed with balances on them, a gym membership that had been charging us for eight months after we'd both stopped going, and a life insurance policy I didn't know my husband had taken out in my name as beneficiary. I also found out I had more in my individual retirement account than I realized. The picture was messier and also better than I thought. You don't know until you look."*

Financial Disclosures ~ The Part You Can't Skip

In most divorce proceedings, both parties are required to submit full financial disclosures ~ a formal, legal accounting of all assets, debts, income, and expenses. This is not optional. It is not something you can approximate or estimate. It is a legal obligation, and submitting inaccurate or incomplete disclosures can have serious legal consequences.

It can also feel deeply exposing. You are laying bare your financial life ~ every mistake, every debt, every embarrassing balance ~ in front of your spouse, their attorney, and potentially a judge. For people who have shame around money, this can feel as vulnerable as anything in the entire divorce process.

Let me offer a reframe: the financial disclosure process is not a judgment of your worth. It is a mechanism for fairness. The court needs accurate information to ensure that both parties walk away from the marriage with a fair share of what was built together. Your debt does not make you a failure. Your dependency does not make you weak. Your financial situation ~ whatever it is ~ is the starting point for what comes next, not a verdict on who you are.

Work closely with your attorney through this process. Make sure every document is accurate and complete. If you discover assets you weren't aware of ~ which happens more often than you might think, particularly in cases involving financial abuse or deliberate concealment ~ tell your attorney immediately. A forensic accountant can be invaluable if you suspect your spouse is hiding assets or income. The cost of hiring one is almost always less than the cost of accepting a settlement based on incomplete information.

Know this: Hiding assets during divorce proceedings is illegal. If you discover your spouse has concealed assets, document everything and tell your attorney. Courts take this seriously.

The Immediate Costs ~ What Divorce Actually Costs

People are often shocked by the immediate financial impact of divorce, and that shock makes an already difficult process even harder. Let's remove the element of surprise.

Legal fees are typically the largest immediate cost. Attorney fees vary enormously by location, complexity, and whether your divorce is contested or uncontested ~ but you should be prepared for retainers ranging from a few thousand dollars to tens of thousands, and total legal costs that can easily run from five figures to six figures in a contested case. This is one of the most important reasons to resolve as much as possible through negotiation and mediation rather than litigation.

Filing fees, court costs, and administrative expenses add up. Mediation fees if you use a mediator. Fees for financial experts, forensic accountants, or custody evaluators if needed. The cost of appraising assets ~ real estate, businesses, collections. All of this is real money leaving your account during a period when your finances are already in flux.

Housing costs are another major immediate reality. If one or both of you needs to move, you're looking at deposits, first and last month's rent, moving costs, and the expense of furnishing a new space from scratch. This is often one of the most underestimated costs of divorce ~ people focus on the legal fees and forget that they may need to completely re-establish a household.

Therapy and mental health support ~ which is absolutely not optional, I will say that clearly ~ is also a cost to plan for. Individual therapy, possible couples therapy if you're in that

phase, support groups. Invest in this. The cost of not investing in your mental health during divorce is measured in years of your life, not dollars.
Build these costs into your financial planning from the beginning. Know what you have available. Know what you can borrow responsibly. Know what your attorney's fees are likely to total. And make a plan ~ even a rough one ~ so that the financial reality of the process doesn't blindside you mid-stream.

Building Your Post-Divorce Budget ~ The New Math

Once you have a clear picture of your financial reality and a sense of what the divorce process will cost, it's time to build your post-divorce budget. Not the budget you wish you had. The budget that is actually achievable given where you are and what you're working with.
Start with your post-divorce income. After the divorce is final, what are your income sources? Your salary or wages. Any alimony or spousal support you'll receive ~ and note: do not build your budget around alimony you're expecting but don't yet have, because support orders can be delayed, disputed, or modified. Child support if applicable, with the same caveat. Any other reliable income.
Then your fixed expenses ~ the ones that don't change month to month. Housing. Car payment if applicable. Insurance premiums. Minimum debt payments. Childcare if applicable. These are non-negotiable. They come first.
Then your variable necessities ~ food, utilities, transportation costs, healthcare out-of-pocket. These can be managed and trimmed but cannot be eliminated.
Then savings. Yes, savings comes before discretionary spending. Even if it's fifty dollars a month. Even if it's twenty-five. Building the habit of paying yourself first ~ before you spend on anything discretionary ~ is one of the single most important financial habits you can establish in your post-divorce life. An emergency fund is not a luxury. It

is the buffer between you and disaster, and you are going to need that buffer.

Then discretionary spending ~ everything else. And this is where you get honest with yourself about what your new reality actually looks like. The subscriptions, the dining out, the clothing, the entertainment. Some of these will need to shrink. Some may need to go entirely, at least for now. This is not forever. This is the season of rebuilding, and rebuilding requires resources.

Marcus: *"The hardest part of building my new budget was accepting that my lifestyle was going to look different for a while. We'd had two incomes and a nice house and vacations. I moved into a one-bedroom apartment and packed my lunch every day for six months. And then something interesting happened ~ I started to feel proud. Not of the sacrifice, but of the fact that I was managing my own money for the first time in twelve years and I was doing it. That apartment felt like freedom even when it felt small."*

Financial Trauma ~ The Part Nobody Talks About

Here is something the financial planning books leave out almost entirely: money is emotional. Deeply, profoundly, sometimes irrationally emotional. And divorce has a way of activating every financial wound you've ever carried ~ your parents' relationship with money, your own history of scarcity or abundance, any ways in which money was used as control or punishment in your marriage.

Financial trauma is real. It shows up as paralysis ~ the inability to open bills, make financial decisions, or even look at your bank balance because the anxiety is overwhelming. It shows up as avoidance ~ spending impulsively to feel some sense of control or pleasure, then feeling shame about it. It shows up as magical thinking ~ believing that things will somehow work out without doing the uncomfortable work of actually making them work out.

If you recognize any of those patterns in yourself, you are not broken and you are not alone. You are a human being navigating one of the most financially destabilizing events of adult life while simultaneously managing enormous grief. Of course your relationship with money is complicated right now.

What helps is naming it. Acknowledging that your financial anxiety is not just about the numbers ~ it's about what the numbers represent. Safety. Control. Independence. The life you thought you were going to have. When you understand that, you can start to separate the emotional response from the practical action. You can feel scared about money and still open the envelope. You can feel overwhelmed by the budget and still sit down and build one.

Working with a financial therapist ~ a professional who sits at the intersection of financial planning and emotional support ~ can be transformative during this period. They exist, they are accessible, and they specialize in exactly the kind of money-and-emotions work that divorce requires. A regular financial planner will give you the numbers. A financial therapist will help you figure out why the numbers make you feel the way they do. Both are valuable. If you can only afford one, talk to a financial planner first. But don't dismiss the emotional work.

And be gentle with yourself during this process. Building a healthy relationship with money after divorce is not a sprint. It is a long, unglamorous, profoundly worthwhile practice of making slightly better decisions, one at a time, until one day you realize you're not afraid anymore.

"Financial peace isn't the acquisition of stuff. It's learning to live on less than you make." ~ Dave Ramsey

Debt ~ Facing It, Managing It, Getting Free of It

Debt is one of the most shame-laden topics in personal finance, and divorce has a way of bringing it into sharp and uncomfortable focus. Whether it's debt you came into the marriage with, debt you accumulated together, or debt you're taking on to fund the divorce itself ~ let's talk about it without flinching.

First, know exactly what you owe. Every balance, every interest rate, every minimum payment. You cannot make a plan to address debt you haven't fully faced. This is the hardest step for most people ~ not because the math is complicated, but because seeing the total number on paper makes it real in a way that's hard to sit with. Sit with it anyway.

Then make a plan. There are two primary strategies for paying down debt, and both work ~ the question is which one works for you. The avalanche method means paying minimums on everything and putting every extra dollar toward the highest-interest debt first. This is mathematically optimal ~ you pay the least total interest over time. The snowball method means paying minimums on everything and putting every extra dollar toward the smallest balance first, regardless of interest rate. This is psychologically powerful ~ each debt you eliminate gives you a win, and wins build momentum.

If you're carrying high-interest credit card debt, explore your options for reducing that interest rate. Balance transfer cards with promotional zero-percent periods can be useful if you're disciplined about paying them down before the promotional period ends. Personal loans at lower interest rates than your cards may be worth considering. Negotiate with creditors directly ~ many will work with you on interest rates or payment plans if you call and ask, especially if you've been a reliable customer.

Protect your credit during this process. Monitor your credit report regularly ~ you're entitled to free reports from all three major bureaus annually, and many credit cards offer free ongoing monitoring. Make sure joint debts that are assigned to your spouse in the settlement are actually transferred out of your name. And if your credit has taken hits during the marriage or the divorce process, know that credit can be rebuilt. It takes time and it takes consistent behavior, but it is absolutely possible.

Important: If you've been financially dependent on your spouse and have little credit history in your own name, begin building your individual credit immediately. Open a credit card in your name. Use it for small purchases. Pay it in full every month. Your future self will thank you.

Long-Term Financial Planning ~ Building What Comes Next

Once you've stabilized the immediate financial picture ~ dealt with the divorce costs, built a working budget, started addressing debt ~ it's time to look further out. Because the goal is not just to survive this period. The goal is to build something genuinely solid on the other side of it.

Retirement savings deserve your attention even when money is tight. If your employer offers a 401(k) match and you are not contributing enough to capture the full match, you are leaving free money on the table. Even a small contribution ~ five or ten percent of your income ~ started early has a compounding effect that cannot be replicated by starting later. If you received a share of your spouse's retirement account in the divorce settlement, understand how it was transferred and what your options are for managing or rolling it over. A financial advisor can help you make the most of these assets.

Emergency fund first, investing second. Before you start putting money into investment accounts, build an emergency fund of three to six months of living expenses in a liquid, accessible savings account. This is your financial immune system. It is what keeps a job loss, a medical bill, or a car repair from becoming a crisis that unravels everything you've worked to build. I know it feels like a long time to save before you start investing. Do it anyway.

Homeownership, if it's a goal for you, is worth planning toward even if it feels distant. Your credit score, your debt-to-income ratio, and your down payment savings are the three levers you control. Work on all three simultaneously. Research first-time homebuyer programs in your state ~ many offer down payment assistance, reduced interest rates, or other benefits that can make homeownership more accessible than you might think.

Insurance is not optional. Life insurance if you have children or dependents who rely on your income. Disability insurance, which most people dramatically underestimate the importance of ~ your ability to earn an income is your most valuable financial asset, and it can be taken away by illness or injury. Health insurance if you were previously covered under your spouse's employer plan ~ losing that coverage is one of the most immediate financial impacts of divorce and needs to be addressed immediately through your own employer, the marketplace, or COBRA.

Estate planning in your own right. A will that reflects your current wishes. Healthcare proxy and power of attorney documents naming people you trust. Beneficiary designations on all accounts updated to reflect your life now, not the life you had. This is not morbid ~ this is responsible. And it is one of the most powerful things you can do to protect yourself and the people you love.

Deja: *"Six months after my divorce was final, I sat down with a financial planner for the first time in my adult life. Just for me. Not us ~ me. She helped me build a five-year plan that included paying off my car, building an emergency fund, and starting to save for a down payment on my own place. Sitting there looking at that plan, I cried. Not because it was sad. Because it was mine. Completely, entirely mine. That feeling is worth every hard month it took to get there."*

A Word on Financial Independence as Liberation

I want to close this chapter with something that doesn't show up in most financial planning guides.

Building your financial independence after divorce is not just a practical exercise. It is an act of self-reclamation. For some of you, this may be the first time in years ~ or ever ~ that you have full visibility into and control over your own finances. For some of you, financial control was something your spouse held over you as power. For some of you, money was a source of such conflict in the marriage that you avoided thinking about it entirely.

Whatever your history with money, this is a new chapter. And in this chapter, you get to decide what your relationship with money looks like. You get to decide what you save for, what you spend on, what you prioritize, what you let go of. No negotiations, no compromises that leave you feeling invisible, no one else's spending habits bleeding into your security.

That is not a small thing. That is enormous.

The work of this chapter is real and sometimes tedious and occasionally terrifying. Do it anyway. Because on the other side of the spreadsheets and the budget meetings and the debt payoff plans is something that feels a lot like freedom. And you have earned every bit of it.

Chapter 5

Healing Is Not Linear Emotional Recovery After Divorce

There was a Tuesday ~ about four months after my divorce was finalized ~ when I woke up feeling genuinely good. Light, even. I made coffee without the usual weight in my chest. I went for a walk and actually looked at the trees. I went to bed that night thinking: okay. Maybe I'm turning the corner.

And then Wednesday arrived and leveled me. Out of nowhere. A song on the radio, a restaurant we used to go to, a stupid inside joke that surfaced in my memory at two in the afternoon in the middle of a grocery store. I stood in the cereal aisle with tears running down my face and a box of cornflakes in my hand, feeling like I had made zero progress and was starting from scratch.

I wasn't starting from scratch. Tuesday was real. Wednesday was also real. Both of them were part of the same healing ~ not a setback and a recovery, but two truths existing simultaneously in the nonlinear, unpredictable, profoundly human process of putting yourself back together after loss.

This chapter is about that process. The real version. Not the version where you cry for a month, then see a therapist, then emerge healed and glowing with hard-won wisdom. The version that actually happens ~ which is messier and longer and more ordinary and ultimately more transformative than anyone's Instagram posts would suggest.

What Grief Actually Looks Like

We talk about grief as though it's a single emotion. It isn't. Grief is a whole weather system ~ and during divorce, you may experience every kind of weather, sometimes within the same afternoon.

There is sadness, of course. The quiet, heavy kind that sits on your chest in the morning. The sharp kind that catches you off guard in public places. The kind that comes not from missing the person specifically but from mourning the life you thought you were going to have ~ the future you'd built in your imagination that no longer exists.

There is anger. White-hot and entirely justified. Anger at your ex, at the situation, at the years that feel wasted, at the version of yourself who didn't see it sooner, at the people who didn't support you, at the ones who took sides. Anger is a healthy part of grief. It is the part that says: I deserved better than this. Honor it. Just don't let it make all your decisions.

There is relief ~ and this one catches people off guard, especially when they feel they're supposed to be sad. If the marriage was painful, if it was suffocating, if you spent years shrinking yourself to fit inside it, then the end of that marriage may bring a relief so profound it frightens you. You may feel guilty about the relief. You may wonder if the relief means you never really loved them. It doesn't. Relief is what the body feels when chronic pain stops. It is a biological response to the end of stress. It is valid.

There is confusion ~ about who you are without this relationship, what you want, what to do with a Saturday afternoon that is suddenly entirely your own. The structure of a marriage, even an unhappy one, provides a kind of scaffolding for daily life. When it comes down, everything feels temporarily formless. That is disorienting. It is also an opening.

There is loneliness. Even if the marriage was deeply lonely. Even if you feel more authentically yourself now than you have in years. Human beings are wired for connection, and the specific connection of a long-term partnership ~ even an imperfect one ~ leaves a particular shape of absence when it's gone.

And there is, eventually, something that starts to feel like possibility. It comes in flickers at first. A morning when you feel curious instead of only sad. A moment when you imagine

something for your future and it doesn't immediately feel like loss. Hold onto those flickers. They are not false. They are what's coming.
Marcus: *"People kept asking me if I was okay, and I kept saying yes because I didn't have the language for what was actually happening. I wasn't okay. But I also wasn't not okay. I was in the middle of something. Something I couldn't name yet. I wish someone had told me that in-between has a name. It's called healing."*

The Grief Nobody Validates ~ LGBTQ+ Divorce Loss

For LGBTQ+ people navigating divorce, there is an additional layer of grief that rarely gets acknowledged ~ and when it isn't acknowledged, it becomes harder to process. Many of us came out into a community that became our entire world. Our social life, our sense of safety, our chosen family, our identity ~ all of it centered in a community that finally felt like home after years of not belonging. When a marriage that was part of that world ends, the grief isn't just about the relationship. It can feel like losing your whole ecosystem.
There is grief for the relationship, yes. But also grief for the shared friend group that may fracture. Grief for the community spaces that now feel complicated to navigate. Grief for the version of yourself that finally felt visible and celebrated, and who now has to figure out who they are in a new configuration. Grief, sometimes, for the identity that was wrapped up in being someone's partner ~ in a community where couplehood can carry enormous weight. And there is a specific grief that belongs to people who came out later in life ~ who came to their identity, and to the right to marry, after years of hiding. For those people, the marriage may have represented something even larger than love. It was proof. Proof that they had arrived. That they were allowed. That all those years of waiting and suppressing and becoming were worth it. When that marriage ends, the grief can feel like losing the proof itself.

You are not losing the proof. Your identity is not contingent on your marital status. Your right to love and be loved is not revoked by divorce. But I understand why it can feel that way, and I want to name it clearly: that grief is real and it deserves to be tended to, not explained away.

Building Your Support Network ~ Who Gets a Seat

Not everyone in your life is equipped to support you through divorce. This is not a judgment of those people ~ grief requires a specific kind of presence that not everyone knows how to offer. Part of healing is getting honest about who in your life can actually show up for you right now, and letting go of the expectation that everyone should.

The seat at your table goes to the people who listen without immediately trying to fix. Who can sit with you in the hard feelings without redirecting you to silver linings before you're ready. Who don't make your divorce about their own discomfort, their own opinions about your ex, their own investment in a particular outcome. Who check in without expecting a performance of recovery from you. Who can hear the messy, unresolved, contradictory truth of what you're experiencing and not flinch.

These people are rare. If you have one of them, protect that relationship. If you have two, you are wealthy in the most important currency. If you're not sure you have any ~ we'll get to that in the chosen family section, because building a support system from scratch is absolutely possible and it is something LGBTQ+ people have been doing masterfully for generations.

Family is complicated during divorce. Some families rally ~ they show up, they listen, they hold you with no strings attached. Others take sides, get wrapped up in their own grief about the marriage ending, or make the process about their own feelings and opinions. Some families, particularly those who were not fully supportive of your relationship to begin with, use the divorce as an opportunity to say things that are damaging under the guise of being right all along.

Know which category your family falls into and adjust your expectations accordingly. You cannot pour from a container that is being simultaneously emptied by the people you're going to for support.

Friends require a similar assessment. Some friendships will deepen during this period ~ the ones that were always real will become realer. Some friendships will reveal themselves to be primarily couple-friendships that don't survive the restructuring. Some friends will be wonderful for the first month and then run out of capacity, not because they don't care but because sustained support is genuinely hard. None of this is a moral verdict on anyone. It is just the reality of who people are and what they can give.

Professional support ~ a therapist, counselor, or divorce coach ~ is not a luxury or a last resort. It is an essential part of a functional support system. We will talk about this in depth shortly. For now, just know: asking for professional help is not a sign that the people in your life aren't enough. It is a sign that you are taking your healing seriously enough to bring in someone who is specifically trained to help.

Deja: *"I had a friend ~ my closest friend, I thought ~ who stopped calling about six weeks in. She didn't disappear entirely, but the calls got shorter and less frequent and I could feel her running out of things to say. It hurt. And then I realized she wasn't equipped for sustained grief. She was great at celebrations and terrible at sitting in darkness. That didn't make her a bad friend. It made her a specific kind of friend. I stopped going to her for what she couldn't give and started going to her for what she could. And I found other people for the rest."*

Chosen Family ~ When Blood Doesn't Show Up

This section is close to my heart. Because for many LGBTQ+ people ~ and for many people regardless of identity who have complicated or absent biological families ~ chosen family is not a consolation prize for the real thing. It is the real thing.

Chosen family is built deliberately, out of love and mutual recognition and the specific kind of trust that comes from choosing each other rather than being assigned to each other. It does not have the built-in history of biological family. But it has something else: the knowledge that every person in that circle chose to be there. That choice means something.

During and after divorce, chosen family can be the structure that holds you when everything else is restructuring. The friend who shows up with groceries without being asked. The mentor who helps you think through decisions without judgment. The found-family dinner table where you are known and wanted and don't have to explain yourself. The group text that starts with a check-in every Monday morning because someone decided to start it and everyone decided to answer.

If you have a chosen family already, lean into them now. Tell them what you need ~ not what you think you should need, not what will make them most comfortable to provide, but what you actually need. People who love you want to help. Most of the time they're waiting to be told how.

If you don't have a chosen family ~ if divorce has left you feeling more isolated than you've ever been, if your support system was tangled up in the marriage and has partially dissolved with it ~ know that you can build one. It takes time. It takes showing up for other people as well as being shown up for. It takes being willing to be known, which requires being willing to be vulnerable, which is hard when you're already raw.

But it is possible. And the places you find it might surprise you. Support groups for people going through divorce ~ both general and LGBTQ+-specific ~ can be a starting point. Community organizations, faith communities if that is part of your life, volunteer work, hobby groups, the neighbor you've waved to for three years and never actually met. Connection is everywhere. It requires only that you reach toward it.

One more thing about chosen family: it includes you. The relationship you have with yourself ~ your ability to be your own source of comfort, your own voice of reason, your own gentle companion in the hard moments ~ is the foundation on which every other relationship is built. We'll come back to this in the self-care section. But start here: you are someone worth choosing. Choose yourself first.

Therapy ~ The Real Talk

Let's be honest about therapy in a way that most books aren't.

Therapy is not magic. A good therapist will not fix you, rescue you, or tell you what to do. What they will do ~ if they are skilled and if the fit is right ~ is give you a space to say the things you cannot say anywhere else. To think out loud without consequences. To be witnessed in your most unpolished, unresolved, contradictory self. And to be guided, gently and skillfully, toward your own clarity.

That is enormously valuable. It is also work. The sessions where you walk out feeling lighter are real. So are the sessions where you walk out feeling cracked open and wrung out and not sure you want to go back. The cracked-open sessions are often the most important ones.

Finding the right therapist matters more than most people realize. The research on therapy outcomes consistently shows that the quality of the relationship between therapist and client ~ called the therapeutic alliance ~ is one of the strongest predictors of whether therapy actually helps. This means if you try a therapist and they don't feel right, you are not obligated to stay. You are not being disloyal or difficult. You are doing exactly what you should do ~ finding the person who can actually help you.

When looking for a therapist, consider specialization. A therapist who specializes in grief, divorce, or life transitions will have a specific toolkit for what you're going through. For LGBTQ+ clients, an affirming therapist is not optional ~ it is a baseline requirement. An affirming therapist is not simply one who won't actively harm you. It is one who understands

LGBTQ+ experience, recognizes the specific stressors that come with navigating the world as an LGBTQ+ person, and does not require you to educate them about your own community before they can help you.

Questions worth asking a potential therapist: What is your experience working with people going through divorce? What is your approach ~ cognitive behavioral, psychodynamic, somatic, EMDR, something else? What does a typical session look like? How do you handle it if I feel like we're not clicking? Do you have experience with LGBTQ+ clients and can you speak to your approach to affirming care?

If cost is a barrier ~ and it often is ~ there are options. Many therapists offer sliding scale fees based on income. Community mental health centers provide low-cost or free services. Online therapy platforms have expanded access significantly and at lower price points than traditional in-person therapy. University training clinics offer therapy provided by supervised graduate students at significantly reduced rates. Open Path Collective is a nonprofit network of therapists who offer reduced-rate sessions specifically for people in financial need. The barrier to therapy is often lower than people assume. It is worth investigating before concluding it is out of reach.

Resource: Psychology Today's therapist finder (psychologytoday.com/us/therapists) allows you to filter by specialty, insurance, sliding scale availability, and LGBTQ+ affirming practice. It is one of the most useful starting points for finding a therapist.

The Toolkit ~ What Actually Helps

Beyond therapy, there is a set of practices that consistently help people navigate the emotional terrain of divorce. These are not revolutionary. They are not particularly glamorous. They work anyway.

Journaling. You do not have to be a writer. You do not have to write eloquently or at length or with any particular structure. You just have to put words somewhere outside your own head. Externalizing thoughts ~ getting them out of the loop of rumination and onto a page ~ creates distance. Distance creates perspective. Perspective creates choice. Write what you're angry about. Write what you're scared of. Write the thing you can't say to anyone. Write the version of yourself you're trying to become. No one has to read it. It is for you.

Movement. The body holds grief in ways the mind cannot always access. Exercise ~ walking, running, swimming, dancing, lifting, yoga, whatever form resonates with you ~ gives the body somewhere to put what it's carrying. It also produces neurochemical changes that genuinely help with mood, anxiety, and sleep. This is not about losing weight or getting a revenge body. It is about taking care of the physical container of your healing. Move it. Regularly. Even when you don't feel like it. Especially when you don't feel like it.

Mindfulness and meditation. I know. You've heard this before. I'm saying it again because it works, and because divorce is one of the conditions it works most powerfully for. The practice of learning to observe your thoughts without being consumed by them ~ of noticing the grief, the anger, the fear, and saying there it is rather than I am drowning in it ~ is a skill that takes time to build and pays dividends for the rest of your life. Start with five minutes. Use an app if you need structure. Be patient with yourself when your mind wanders, which it will, constantly, because that is what minds do.

Routine. When the structure of a shared life dissolves, creating your own structure is an act of self-care. A morning routine that is yours. A regular bedtime. Meals at consistent times. These things sound small and feel enormous when everything else is in flux. Routine tells your nervous system: this is predictable. This is safe. You are okay. Give your nervous system that message as often as you can.

Rest. Genuine rest. Not the exhausted collapse of someone who has been running from their feelings all day. Actual, deliberate rest ~ sufficient sleep, time to do nothing, permission to not be productive. Grief is metabolically expensive. Your body is doing significant work even when you feel like you're just sitting there. Let it rest.

Creative expression. Writing, painting, music, cooking, gardening, building things ~ any form of making something out of raw material. Creativity during grief is not about producing anything worth showing anyone. It is about the process of transforming formless feeling into something with shape. It is one of the most ancient and effective forms of emotional processing that exists.

Community. Showing up for other people ~ a support group, volunteer work, a community organization, a friend who needs help ~ is not a distraction from your healing. It is part of it. Being in service to others reminds you that your world is larger than your pain. It generates connection. It gives you evidence of your own capacity and worth at a time when both can feel uncertain.

Marcus: *"I started running three months after my divorce was filed. I'd never been a runner. I hated running. But I needed somewhere to put the anger and the grief and the adrenaline of all of it, and running was free and available at six in the morning when the feelings were loudest. By the time the divorce was final I'd run a 5K. Not because I cared about the race. Because I needed proof that I could do hard things. That race was proof."*

Rumination ~ When Your Own Mind Becomes the Problem

Rumination is what happens when grief gets stuck. Instead of moving through you, it loops. The same thoughts, the same questions, the same what-ifs and if-onlys, cycling endlessly without resolution. It is exhausting. It is also extremely common during divorce, and it is worth understanding specifically so you can interrupt it.

Rumination feels productive because it feels like thinking. You are going over the details, analyzing what went wrong, trying to understand. But unlike genuine reflection ~ which moves toward insight and resolution ~ rumination just circles. It does not deliver answers because it is not actually seeking them. It is the mind's way of trying to control something that cannot be controlled by thinking about it harder.

The antidote to rumination is not willpower. It is not telling yourself to stop thinking about it, which works about as well as telling yourself not to think about a pink elephant. The antidote is interruption and redirection. When you notice you are in the loop ~ and noticing is the first skill to develop ~ you interrupt it with something that requires your full attention. Physical movement works well because it pulls the nervous system out of its loop. A task that requires focus. A conversation with someone who grounds you. Anything that brings you fully into the present moment and out of the endless replay of the past.

Therapy is particularly useful for rumination because a skilled therapist can help you identify the underlying need that the rumination is trying to meet ~ often a need for certainty, or control, or closure ~ and find more effective ways to address it. If your rumination is severe enough to significantly impair your sleep, your work, your relationships, or your daily functioning, that is worth discussing with both a therapist and a physician. Sometimes what presents as rumination has a neurological or biochemical component that responds to treatment.

Giving Yourself Grace ~ The Practice

I want to end this chapter with something that sounds simple and is actually one of the hardest practices in this entire book.

Give yourself grace.

Not as a platitude. Not as a thing you say to yourself and then immediately contradict with a list of all the ways you should be further along, doing better, feeling less, needing less. As an actual practice. A daily, deliberate, sometimes effortful choice to treat yourself with the same patience and compassion you would offer a person you love who is going through exactly what you are going through.

Because here is what I know about the people who read books like this one: you are harder on yourself than you are on anyone else. You hold yourself to a standard of recovery and resilience that you would never impose on a friend. You apologize for needing things. You minimize what you're going through because someone else has it worse. You push through when you should rest. You perform okayness when you are not okay. You measure your grief against a timeline that someone or something has told you it should fit inside. It doesn't fit inside a timeline. Healing doesn't work that way. And the energy you spend judging yourself for not being healed faster is energy that could be going toward the actual healing.

So this is the practice: notice the self-judgment when it comes. And then ~ not by pretending it isn't there, not by suppressing it, but by gently, firmly redirecting ~ offer yourself what you would offer someone you love. Some patience. Some acknowledgment of how hard this actually is. Some reminder that you are doing the best you can with what you have in a genuinely difficult season. Some credit for still being here, still trying, still reaching toward something better.

You are healing. It doesn't always look like healing. It doesn't always feel like healing. But you are reading this book, which means you are still moving toward something. That matters more than you know.

"You yourself, as much as anybody in the entire universe, deserve your love and affection." ~ Sharon Salzberg

Tend to yourself. The rest will follow.

Chapter 6

Co-Parenting Without Losing Your Mind

Let me say something that co-parenting books rarely say out loud:

Co-parenting with someone you are divorcing ~ someone who may have hurt you, betrayed you, frustrated you for years, or simply become a stranger ~ is one of the hardest things a human being can be asked to do. It requires you to show up professionally and cooperatively for a person you may be actively grieving, actively furious at, or actively trying to emotionally distance yourself from. It requires you to compartmentalize in ways that feel unnatural and sometimes deeply unfair. It requires you to put someone else's needs ~ your child's needs ~ ahead of your own feelings, repeatedly, on days when your own feelings are enormous.

It is hard. I will not pretend otherwise.

And it is also one of the most important things you will ever do. Because your children are watching. Not just watching what you do ~ watching what you model. About relationships, about conflict, about how adults treat each other when things are hard. About whether love is something that endures restructuring or something that curdles into cruelty when it ends. What you show them in this season will live in them for decades.

That is not pressure. That is purpose. And purpose, on the hard days, is what keeps you showing up.

Your Children Are Not Messengers, Spies, or Therapists

Before we get into the practical architecture of co-parenting, let's establish the non-negotiables. The things that, no matter how angry you are, no matter how justified your feelings, no matter what your ex has done ~ you simply do not do. Not because your ex deserves your restraint. Because your children deserve your protection.

Do not use your children as messengers. If you need to communicate something to your co-parent, communicate it directly ~ by text, email, app, or phone call. Sending information through your child puts them in the middle of something they should never be in the middle of. It also puts them in the position of worrying about whether they delivered the message correctly, whether it caused a conflict, whether they are somehow responsible for the communication between their parents. They are not responsible. They are children. Keep them out of it.

Do not use your children as spies. Asking your child what the other parent's house is like, who comes over, what they talk about, whether they're seeing anyone ~ this is information-gathering dressed up as parenting. Your children will feel the purpose underneath the question even if they can't name it. It creates loyalty conflicts that are deeply damaging. What happens in the other household is not your business unless it directly threatens your child's safety. If there are genuine safety concerns, address them through your attorney, not through your eight-year-old.

Do not use your children as therapists. They cannot hold your grief. They should not have to. Your sadness, your anger, your loneliness, your fear ~ these belong in your journal, in your therapy sessions, in conversations with your adult support network. When you cry in front of your children about the divorce in ways that make them feel responsible for your emotional state, you are asking them to carry something that is not theirs to carry. They love you. They will try to carry it. And it will cost them something.

Do not speak negatively about your co-parent in front of your children. This one is hard ~ especially when what you want to say is true. Especially when you are furious and exhausted and your ex has done something infuriating and your child is right there. Do not do it. Your child is made of both of you. When you attack your co-parent in front of them, some part of what you're saying lands on them too. Protect them from that.

Deja: *"There was a night ~ maybe two months after we separated ~ when my daughter asked me why Daddy didn't live with us anymore. She was six. And I had this wave of wanting to tell her exactly why. All of it. The truth. I wanted her to know. And then I looked at her little face and I thought: she loves him. She is allowed to love him. That is not my war to bring to her. I said, 'Sometimes grown-ups decide to live in different houses so everyone can be happier.' She thought about it and said, 'Is Daddy happier?' And I said, 'I think so, baby.' That was one of the hardest things I've ever done. It was also the right thing."*

Building Your Co-Parenting Plan ~ The Architecture of Two Homes

A co-parenting plan is a formal document ~ typically filed with the court as part of your divorce agreement ~ that establishes the structure of how you and your co-parent will raise your children across two households. It is worth taking seriously and getting right, because a well-built co-parenting plan reduces conflict, provides stability for your children, and gives you a framework to return to when things get hard.

Physical custody ~ where your child lives and when ~ is the foundation of the plan. Common arrangements include equal or near-equal time-sharing, primary residence with one parent and visitation for the other, or various hybrid arrangements that work around specific schedules and needs. There is no universally right answer. The right answer depends on your children's ages and needs, your geographic proximity to each other, work schedules, school logistics, and the overall quality of the co-parenting relationship.

Legal custody ~ the right to make major decisions about your child's upbringing ~ is typically shared jointly even when physical custody is not equal. This means both parents have a say in decisions about education, healthcare, religious upbringing, and extracurricular activities. Joint legal custody requires communication and compromise. If your co-parenting relationship is too damaged for that, sole legal custody may be appropriate and your attorney can advise you on the standards in your state.

Holiday and vacation scheduling deserves specific attention in your plan because it is one of the most consistent sources of conflict in co-parenting relationships. Who has the children on Thanksgiving, Christmas, Hanukkah, Eid, Mother's Day, Father's Day, birthdays, school breaks, and summer vacation ~ all of it should be spelled out clearly and in advance. Many plans alternate major holidays on an annual basis. Build this structure before the first holiday season arrives, not during it.

A communication protocol is worth including. How will you communicate about your children ~ by text, email, a co-parenting app? What is the expected response time for non-urgent matters? What constitutes an emergency that warrants an immediate call? What decisions require mutual agreement versus what each parent can make independently in their own household? Establishing these norms in writing, when things are calm, saves enormous conflict later.

A process for handling disagreements is also worth building in. When you and your co-parent cannot agree on something ~ and you will, at some point, not be able to agree on something ~ what happens? Mediation first? A specific family therapist who knows your situation? The plan itself becomes the referee when emotions are high.

Tool worth knowing: Co-parenting apps like OurFamilyWizard, TalkingParents, and Cozi are specifically designed to help divorced parents communicate and coordinate without the emotional charge of direct personal communication. They track messages, create shared calendars, manage expense logs, and provide a documented record that can be used in court if needed. If direct communication with your co-parent is consistently difficult, these tools can be genuinely transformative.

Communicating With Your Co-Parent ~ Without Going Feral

This is the section I probably needed most during my own divorce. Because communicating with someone who has hurt you, or who you have hurt, or who simply knows exactly which buttons to push ~ while maintaining the kind of calm, child-focused professionalism that your kids need from you ~ is a skill. And like all skills, it can be learned.

The most useful mindset shift I found was this: treat your co-parent like a difficult colleague. Not a friend. Not an enemy. A colleague. Someone with whom you have a shared professional obligation ~ the raising of your children ~ and with whom you interact as needed, as civilly as possible, and no more than necessary. You do not have to like this colleague. You do not have to forgive them yet. You do not have to pretend the history isn't there. You simply have to work with them, because the project ~ your children ~ requires it.

Keep communications child-focused. If it is not about your child's schedule, health, education, or well-being, it probably does not need to be said in a co-parenting communication. The divorce, the feelings, the grievances ~ those live elsewhere. When you open a co-parenting app or sit down to write an email about pickup time, the only topic on the table is the children.

Keep communications brief and factual. Not cold ~ brief. Not hostile ~ factual. State what you need to communicate, confirm what needs to be confirmed, and close the communication. Long messages invite long responses. Emotional messages invite emotional responses. The shorter and more neutral your communication, the less surface area there is for conflict.

Give yourself a pause before responding to anything that provokes you. When your co-parent sends a message that makes your blood pressure rise ~ and they will, because they know you well enough to know exactly how ~ do not respond immediately. Walk away from your phone. Do something physical. Give yourself twenty minutes, or an hour, or until tomorrow morning. Then respond from the calmer version of yourself, not the activated one. The calm response is almost always the one you will be glad you sent.

Use the BIFF method when things get charged: Brief, Informative, Friendly, and Firm. Brief because long messages escalate. Informative because your communication needs to convey what it needs to convey. Friendly ~ not warmly friendly, professionally friendly ~ because it models maturity and does not give your co-parent ammunition. Firm because you have needs and boundaries that are legitimate and worth holding.

Document everything that matters. If you have a co-parent who is unreliable, who frequently deviates from the plan, who makes agreements verbally and then denies them later ~ get it in writing. Use the co-parenting app. Follow up verbal conversations with a brief confirming message. Not because you are building a case against them, but because documentation protects you and provides clarity for everyone, including the children.

Marcus: *"The thing that saved me was switching to OurFamilyWizard after the first three months. Before that, we were texting, and every text felt like a landmine. He'd say something that had nothing to do with our son and everything to do with our marriage and I would respond and it would spiral. The app changed the energy entirely. There was something about the format ~ the shared calendar, the fact that everything was documented ~ that made both of us behave better. It was like having a referee in the room who never said anything but whose presence kept things civil."*

When Your Co-Parent Makes It Hard ~ Navigating High-Conflict Situations

Everything in the previous section assumes a co-parent who is difficult but ultimately willing to participate in a functional co-parenting relationship. Not every situation looks like that. Some co-parents are not difficult ~ they are genuinely high-conflict, and the distinction matters.

A high-conflict co-parent may consistently violate the custody agreement and then minimize or deny it. They may use the children as weapons ~ withholding them, badmouthing you relentlessly, making drop-offs and pickups into scenes. They may use communication as a vehicle for harassment, sending messages that are designed to provoke or control. They may make false allegations. They may involve the children in adult conflicts in ways that are genuinely harmful.

If this is your situation, the standard co-parenting advice does not fully apply. You cannot co-parent collaboratively with someone who is not acting in good faith. What you can do is parallel parent ~ a model where each parent operates independently in their own household, interaction between parents is minimized as much as possible, and all communication goes through formal channels. You are not co-parenting together. You are each parenting separately, with the child moving between two distinct environments.

Document every violation of the custody agreement. Every missed pickup, every late return, every communication that crosses a line. Dates, times, what happened, any witnesses. This documentation is not paranoia ~ it is protection. Family courts make decisions based on patterns, and patterns require records.

If your co-parent's behavior is rising to the level of harassment, parental alienation, or endangerment of your children, talk to your attorney. Court orders can be modified. Custody arrangements can be changed when a parent's behavior demonstrably harms the children. The legal system is not a perfect tool but it is a tool, and you are entitled to use it.

And finally ~ get support. Co-parenting with a high-conflict individual is a specific kind of sustained stress that requires its own kind of support. A therapist who understands high-conflict divorce and co-parenting, a support group of people in similar situations, close trusted friends who can help you decompress without judgment. You cannot sustain this alone. Don't try.

LGBTQ+-Specific Co-Parenting ~ The Unique Terrain

LGBTQ+ co-parenting after divorce carries specific challenges that the standard parenting books don't address. Let's name them clearly.

Non-biological parental rights are the most urgent issue for many LGBTQ+ families. If you are a non-biological parent who did not complete a second-parent adoption or establish legal parentage through other means, your rights to your child may be legally precarious ~ particularly if your co-parent decides to use that vulnerability against you during divorce proceedings. This is one of the most painful realities of LGBTQ+ family law, and it is one of the most important reasons to consult an LGBTQ+-specialized family law attorney as early as possible in the process. Courts in many states are increasingly recognizing the parental rights of non-biological parents who have functioned as parents, but the legal landscape varies significantly by state and the outcome is never guaranteed without documentation.

If you are the biological parent in this situation, I want to speak to you directly: using your biological status as a weapon against your co-parent is a choice that will harm your children. Your child's other parent ~ the one who changed diapers at 3 a.m., who showed up for every school play, who loved them from before they could speak ~ is their parent. Regardless of what is or is not on a birth certificate. Erasing that parent from your child's life to gain legal leverage is not a co-parenting strategy. It is a wound you are inflicting on your child that they will carry for the rest of their life.

Talking to your children about your identity during and after divorce requires thoughtfulness that varies by your child's age, your specific family history, and what the child already knows. If your child is aware of your LGBTQ+ identity, maintain open, age-appropriate conversations about what makes your family unique and wonderful. If the divorce has brought your identity more publicly into focus ~ if you came out more fully as part of your decision to end the marriage ~

navigate that disclosure carefully, with the support of a therapist if possible, and always leading with love and reassurance.

Your child's school, healthcare providers, and community should be made aware of the new family structure and, where relevant, the legal custody arrangement. Make sure both parents are listed on school emergency contacts and medical forms where legally appropriate. If your co-parent has full legal custody rights, they are entitled to information and access. If they do not, make sure the relevant institutions know that.

Community support for your children matters. LGBTQ+ family organizations, PFLAG chapters, school GSAs, and online communities for children of LGBTQ+ parents can provide your children with peers who understand their family experience. Children who feel that their family is not invisible ~ who have community that reflects and celebrates their reality ~ are significantly more resilient. Connect them to that community wherever you can find it.

And for yourself ~ find your co-parenting community. Other LGBTQ+ parents navigating divorce and co-parenting exist, and they have walked terrain that is specific to your experience in ways that general parenting groups cannot fully address. Online communities, LGBTQ+ family centers, and therapy groups specifically for LGBTQ+ parents in transition are worth seeking out. You should not have to translate your experience before you can receive support.

Marcus: *"My son was nine when we separated. He already knew I was gay ~ he'd grown up with two dads. What he didn't understand was why two dads who loved him couldn't still live together. That question broke my heart every time he asked it. We eventually found a therapist who worked specifically with children of divorcing same-sex parents. She had language for it that I didn't have. She helped him understand that families can change shape and still be families. That love doesn't require a floor plan. I will be grateful for her forever."*

Encouraging Healthy Children Through Divorce ~ What the Research Says

Let's end with the research. Because when things feel impossible, it helps to know what actually works.

The research on children and divorce is nuanced and often misrepresented. The headline that divorce automatically damages children is not supported by the evidence. What the evidence actually shows is that the quality of the co-parenting relationship ~ specifically, the level of conflict children are exposed to ~ is one of the strongest predictors of children's outcomes after divorce. Children whose parents divorce but maintain a low-conflict, cooperative co-parenting relationship do significantly better than children whose parents stay together in a high-conflict household.

Let that land for a moment. It is not the divorce that damages children most. It is the conflict. Which means your effort to build a functional, civil, child-focused co-parenting relationship ~ even when it is hard, even when it is deeply unfair, even when it requires more grace than you feel you have ~ is one of the most powerful investments in your child's well-being you can make.

Children are also remarkably resilient when they have consistent access to both parents, when the adults in their lives are emotionally stable and available to them, when their daily routines remain as consistent as possible, and when they feel free to love both parents without guilt or pressure. These things are within your control. Focus your energy there.

Finally ~ your own healing matters for your children. A parent who is getting therapy, building a support network, and doing the work of their own recovery is a better parent than one who is white-knuckling it alone. Taking care of yourself is not selfish. It is what makes you available to take care of them. You cannot pour from an empty cup, and no one knows that more acutely than a divorced parent doing the daily work of showing up.

"The goal of co-parenting is not to make your ex happy. It is to make your children whole." ~ Unknown

Your children are watching you rebuild. They are learning from every choice you make about how people handle hard things. Show them that hard things can be handled with integrity. With grace. With love that doesn't require a perfect situation to keep showing up.

That is the most important thing you will ever teach them.

Chapter 7

Who Am I Now? Rebuilding Your Identity

Here is a question nobody prepares you for:
Who are you when you are no longer someone's spouse?
It sounds like it should have an easy answer. You are still you ~ your name, your job, your family, your history. You existed before this marriage and you exist after it. Simple.
Except it isn't simple at all. Because identity is not just the facts of who you are. It is the story you tell about who you are. And for years ~ maybe decades ~ that story has included another person. Their preferences shaped your weekends. Their family became part of your family. Your social world was built around a partnership. Your future was imagined as a we. And now the story needs to be rewritten with a different pronoun, and nobody handed you the pen.
This chapter is about finding the pen. About the specific, unglamorous, occasionally thrilling work of figuring out who you are ~ fully, completely, on your own terms ~ after a marriage ends. It is one of the most disorienting chapters of divorce. It is also, if you let it be, one of the most revelatory.

The Identity Audit ~ Taking Stock of Who You've Become

Long-term relationships change us. This is not always a bad thing ~ the best relationships expand us, challenge us, introduce us to parts of ourselves we might not have found alone. But they also, sometimes, shrink us. We accommodate. We compromise. We let go of things that mattered to us because they didn't matter to our partner, or because the relationship required a version of us that didn't include them, or because over time we simply forgot they were there.

The identity audit is the process of figuring out what is still yours ~ what has always been fundamentally you ~ and what you quietly gave up somewhere along the way.

Start with the easy questions. What did you love before this relationship that you stopped doing during it? Hobbies, interests, friendships, habits ~ things that were clearly yours before they got absorbed into the shared life. These are often the easiest places to start reclaiming yourself, because the path back to them is relatively clear. The painting supplies in the back of the closet. The friend you drifted from because your spouse never liked him. The music you stopped playing because it wasn't their taste. Go back to those things. Not because they will instantly feel the same ~ they won't. But because they are breadcrumbs back to yourself.

Then the harder questions. Who did you become in this marriage ~ and how much of that was authentically you? Were there ways you made yourself smaller to keep the peace? Ways you abandoned opinions, desires, or needs because expressing them caused conflict? Ways you performed a version of yourself that your partner preferred, and gradually lost track of the version you actually were? These questions require honesty and some gentleness with yourself. You were not weak for accommodating. You were human. But now is the time to look clearly at what accommodating cost you.

And the hardest question of all: what do you want? Not what you wanted when you got married. Not what you've been conditioned to want by years of being someone's partner. What do you actually, genuinely, for-yourself want ~ from your days, your relationships, your work, your home, your body, your future? Most people going through divorce have not asked themselves this question in a very long time. It is worth sitting with. It does not require an immediate answer. But it requires asking.

Deja: *"I realized about six months after my divorce that I had not chosen a single restaurant in four years. My ex was particular about food and I'd just started defaulting to what he wanted. It sounds small. But when I noticed it, I cried.*

Not because of the restaurants ~ because of what the restaurants represented. All the tiny ways I'd been disappearing. I started eating wherever I wanted. By myself sometimes, which felt radical at first and then felt like freedom."

The Discomfort of Formlessness ~ And Why It's Actually Good

There is a period after divorce ~ it varies in length, but most people experience it ~ that feels like being unmoored. The structure of the shared life is gone. The role of spouse is gone. The future you had mapped out is gone. And what remains feels formless. Like standing in a room where all the furniture has been removed and you're not sure yet what you want to put back.

This is deeply uncomfortable. Human beings are meaning-making creatures and we are most comfortable when we have a clear story about who we are and where we're going. Formlessness disrupts that story. It can feel like identity loss, like failure, like proof that something is fundamentally wrong.

It is none of those things. It is potential.

The empty room is not a punishment. It is an invitation. Every choice you make about what goes back into that room is a choice you are making deliberately, for yourself, without having to negotiate it with anyone. The furniture of your new life ~ your routines, your relationships, your values in action, your daily pleasures, your ambitions ~ gets to be chosen by you. Entirely. That is an extraordinary thing, even when it doesn't feel that way.

The trick is to resist the urge to fill the room immediately. To rush into a new relationship, a new city, a dramatic reinvention that is less about genuine self-discovery and more about escaping the discomfort of not knowing yet. The not-knowing is where the real work happens. Sit in it a little longer than is comfortable. Let yourself be formless for a season. What emerges from that space, when you're patient with it, is more authentically you than anything you could have constructed in a hurry.

Marcus: *"People kept asking me what my plan was. What was I going to do now. And for the first time in my adult life, I didn't have a plan. I'd always had a plan. A five-year plan, a ten-year plan, a spreadsheet of milestones. And the absence of a plan terrified me until I started to realize it was also the first time I could build a plan that was entirely mine. That took a while to feel like a gift. It does feel like a gift now."*

Reconnecting With Your Values ~ The Compass Underneath Everything

Values are not the same as preferences. Preferences are what you like. Values are what you live by ~ the principles that, when you honor them, make you feel like yourself, and when you violate them, leave you feeling hollow and ashamed even if you can't articulate exactly why.

Divorce has a way of clarifying values with remarkable precision, because it strips away the compromises and accommodations and forces you to look at what's actually left. What mattered to you so much that you felt its absence acutely during the marriage? What did you find yourself protecting even when everything else felt negotiable? What are the things you know, with bone-deep certainty, you will not compromise on in the next chapter of your life?

Those answers are your values. And they are the compass for everything that comes next ~ the relationships you build, the work you pursue, the community you seek, the goals you set, the life you design.

Common values that come into sharp focus after divorce: authenticity ~ the need to be genuinely yourself in your relationships rather than performing a version of yourself. Freedom ~ the ability to make choices about your own life without requiring permission or managing someone else's reaction. Growth ~ a commitment to continuing to learn and expand and become. Connection ~ deep, real, reciprocal relationships that nourish rather than deplete. Security ~

emotional, financial, physical stability. Contribution ~ the sense that your existence makes things better for others. Adventure ~ the aliveness that comes from new experiences and unknown territory.

You probably feel several of these. Rank them. Know which ones are non-negotiable. Because when you are clear on your values, decision-making becomes significantly simpler ~ not easy, but clearer. Does this relationship honor my values? Does this opportunity align with what I actually care about? Does this choice move me toward or away from the life I'm building? The values answer those questions when the emotions are too loud to think straight.

Rebuilding Your Community ~ Finding Your People

One of the quietest losses of divorce is social. The couple-friends who drift because couple-friend dynamics don't survive restructuring. The family members who take sides or simply don't know how to relate to you outside the context of your marriage. The community spaces ~ a church, a neighborhood, a social circle ~ that were built around the partnership and now feel complicated to navigate alone.

Rebuilding your social world after divorce is real work. It requires putting yourself in places where connection is possible, which requires vulnerability at a time when you are already raw. It requires being willing to begin again with people who don't know your history, which can feel both liberating and exhausting. It requires patience with the pace of real friendship, which is slower and less dramatic than the movies suggest.

Start where you already are. The colleagues you've been meaning to get to know better. The neighbor you always meant to invite for coffee. The acquaintance from the gym or the book club or the volunteer shift who has always seemed interesting. These are not the friendships of a lifetime necessarily, but they are the beginning of something, and beginnings are what you're building right now.

Find your interest communities. The thing that is truest about adult friendship is that shared interest is the most reliable engine for genuine connection. Join the hiking group, the pottery class, the book club, the choir, the recreational sports league, the gaming night, the community garden. Show up consistently. Be genuinely curious about the people there. Let things develop at their own pace. This is how real friendship is built in adulthood ~ slowly, through repeated proximity and genuine interest in other human beings.

Seek out communities that specifically reflect your experience. For LGBTQ+ people rebuilding after divorce, this means finding spaces where your identity is not an asterisk, where your family structure is not something to explain, where your specific experience of love and loss and community is understood without translation. LGBTQ+ community centers, affirming faith communities, LGBTQ+-specific support groups and social organizations ~ these spaces exist in most cities and increasingly online. They offer the particular gift of being known before you've even introduced yourself.

And be willing to invest in community, not just receive it. Show up for other people. Remember the details of what they've told you and ask about them later. Offer your time, your skills, your presence. Be the person who follows up, who checks in, who shows up when someone is struggling. Community is not a service you subscribe to. It is something you build through reciprocal care, and the more you give to it, the more it becomes genuinely yours.

Deja: *"I joined a pottery class eight months after my divorce. I'd always wanted to try it and never had because it was my thing, not our thing. The first day I walked in I knew no one. By the third week I had exchanged numbers with two women who became real friends. One of them went through her own divorce two years later and called me at midnight from a parking lot. I was there. That's what community does ~ it creates the web that catches you. But you have to weave it first."*

Setting New Goals ~ Building a Vision That's Actually Yours

Goal-setting after divorce is different from the goal-setting you may have done within the marriage. Those goals were negotiated, shared, shaped by the compromise of two people with two sets of desires trying to build one life. These goals are different. These are yours alone.

That freedom can be paralyzing at first. When you can go anywhere, how do you choose a direction? When no one else's needs constrain your choices, what do you actually want? Start smaller than you think you need to. You do not need a five-year plan right now. You need a next-three-months intention. Something specific enough to move toward, achievable enough to feel like progress, meaningful enough to get you out of bed on the mornings when staying in bed feels easier.

Personal goals might look like: finishing the degree you put on hold, starting a fitness practice and sticking with it for six months, reading twenty books this year, learning to cook five new dishes, taking a solo trip somewhere you've always wanted to go, or simply establishing a morning routine that starts your day feeling like yours rather than reactive.

Professional goals might look like: pursuing the promotion you've been hesitant about, pivoting to a field that actually interests you, starting the side project you've been gestating for years, going back to school, or simply negotiating a raise you deserve and have been too distracted to ask for.

Relational goals might look like: deepening three existing friendships intentionally, reconnecting with a family member you've lost touch with, joining a community that reflects your values, or working toward a healthier relationship with yourself ~ which is, arguably, the foundational relational goal of this entire season.

Use the SMART framework if structure helps you: Specific, Measurable, Achievable, Relevant, Time-bound. But don't let the framework become the point. The point is motion. Forward, intentional, self-directed motion. After years of shared direction, choosing your own direction ~ even imperfectly, even with uncertainty ~ is an act of profound self-reclamation.

And build in celebration. Not grand, performative celebration ~ quiet acknowledgment of your own progress. You paid off the credit card. You finished the class. You went to the pottery studio for the twelfth week in a row even though last Tuesday you really didn't want to. These are not small things. They are evidence of who you are becoming. Collect that evidence. You will need it on the harder days.

The New Interests ~ Permission to Begin Again

One of the quiet gifts of rebuilding your identity after divorce is this: you get to try things. Without justification. Without negotiation. Without the silent weight of a partner's disinterest or the logistics of coordinating with another person's schedule and preferences. You get to just try things, for no reason other than curiosity.

This sounds simple. It feels enormous when you've spent years in a relationship where your individual interests required explanation or justification or compromise. The first time you sign up for something just because you want to ~ just because it looked interesting and you thought why not ~ and then go without asking anyone's permission or checking anyone's calendar, is a quietly radical act of self-possession.

Try things that feel unlike you. The version of you that existed in your marriage may have been defined by certain things ~ certain tastes, certain habits, certain ways of spending time ~ that were as much about the relationship as about you. Step outside those definitions. Try the thing that your married self would have said wasn't really your kind of thing. You might be surprised. Or you might confirm that it actually isn't your thing ~ and that's useful information too.

Try things that scare you a little. Not recklessly ~ but that edge of mild fear that signals you are stretching. The improv class. The solo travel. The creative project you've been telling yourself you're not talented enough for. The conversation with a stranger that you actually follow through on instead of

letting the moment pass. Fear at that level is usually a sign that something matters ~ that it means enough to be worth being afraid of.
And try things slowly. You do not have to reinvent yourself by next Tuesday. Identity is not a renovation project with a deadline. It is a lifelong process of becoming, and divorce simply gives you an unusual amount of raw material to work with at once. Take your time. Be curious rather than urgent. Let yourself be a beginner at things. Beginners are people who are still open to being surprised by what they discover.
Marcus: *"I took a ceramics class. I was terrible at it. I am still terrible at it two years later. I go every Thursday evening and I make lopsided bowls that no one would want to eat from and I come home filthy and happy and it has nothing to do with anything useful or productive or marketable and it is one of the best things I do for myself. Nobody needed me to be good at ceramics. I just needed something that was entirely, stupidly, joyfully mine."*

Embracing Change ~ The Longer View

Identity is not a destination. It is a direction. And the direction you are moving in right now ~ toward greater authenticity, toward a life that is genuinely yours, toward a self that has been tempered by loss and is stronger and clearer for it ~ is one of the most meaningful directions a person can travel.
Change after divorce is not optional. The question is only whether you move through it consciously or whether it happens to you. The people who emerge from divorce most whole are the ones who chose the change ~ who looked at the rubble and said: I get to decide what goes back in this room. Who asked the hard questions about who they had been and who they wanted to become. Who were willing to sit in the discomfort of not knowing long enough for something real to surface.
You are not the person you were when this marriage started. You are also not the person you were on the day it ended. You are in the process of becoming someone else ~ someone

who has loved and lost and survived and learned things about themselves that comfort and ease could never have taught them.

That person is worth getting to know. Make the time. Do the work. Stay curious.

The world does not need the version of you that was made for someone else. It needs the version of you that was made for yourself. That version is in there. This chapter of your life is the work of finding them.

"The privilege of a lifetime is to become who you truly are." ~ Carl Jung

Go find out who that is.

You have the rest of your life, and it starts right now.

Chapter 8

Back in the Game
Dating After Divorce

Let's start with the thing everyone is secretly wondering but nobody wants to ask first:

Am I ready to date again?

And the honest answer ~ the one I wish someone had given me ~ is that readiness is not a destination you arrive at. It is not a box you check after completing a sufficient amount of grief work. It is not a feeling that descends on you one morning like clarity from the heavens, letting you know that you are healed enough, whole enough, done enough processing to let another human being in.

Readiness is a practice. You become ready by doing the work ~ the identity work, the emotional work, the values clarification ~ and then by taking careful, intentional steps back toward connection when something in you is genuinely curious rather than just lonely or afraid.

The distinction between lonely and ready matters enormously. Lonely reaches for anything warm. Ready reaches for something real. And if you have been doing the work of the previous chapters ~ if you have been building your identity, your community, your financial stability, your emotional toolkit ~ you are closer to ready than you probably feel.

This chapter will not tell you when to date. That is yours to know. What it will do is prepare you to date well ~ to show up for new relationships as the person you are becoming rather than as the person still haunted by who you were. That distinction is everything.

The Emotional Baggage Claim ~ What You're Carrying In

Every person who has been through a divorce walks into their next relationship carrying something. This is not a flaw.

It is the reality of being a human being with a history. The question is not whether you are carrying anything ~ you are ~ but whether you know what it is.

Because baggage you haven't named is baggage that operates invisibly. It shows up as the disproportionate reaction to something your new partner said that touched an old wound. The hair-trigger defensiveness about a topic that was a battleground in your marriage. The way you brace for abandonment in moments that don't actually threaten it. The walls you've built that are so solid you can't always tell where protection ends and isolation begins.

Take inventory. What did your marriage teach you ~ accurately or not ~ about relationships? Maybe it taught you that vulnerability gets punished, so you now protect yourself by staying slightly surface-level even with people who have earned more. Maybe it taught you that your needs are too much, so you minimize them until they explode. Maybe it taught you that love requires constant management and management is exhausting, so you now find intimacy anxiety-producing rather than nourishing. Maybe it taught you that you cannot trust your own judgment about people ~ and that one is particularly corrosive, because it makes every new relationship feel like standing on ice you're not sure will hold.

Name these things. Not to shame yourself for having them ~ they are reasonable responses to real experiences. But to see them clearly enough that you can choose how to respond to them rather than being driven by them without realizing it.

Therapy before dating is not mandatory but it is genuinely useful ~ specifically the kind of therapy that helps you understand your relational patterns. How do you attach? Do you tend toward anxious attachment, chasing reassurance and reading threat into normal distance? Avoidant attachment, pulling away from closeness right when it starts to feel real? Disorganized attachment, oscillating between desperate connection and terrified retreat? Understanding your attachment style is one of the most useful pieces of self-knowledge you can carry into a new relationship, because it tells you where your blind spots are before they become someone else's problem.

Deja: *"My therapist called it my 'proof-seeking' pattern. Anytime I started to feel close to someone new, I would unconsciously start looking for evidence that they were going to betray me. I'd overanalyze texts. I'd test them without telling them they were being tested. I'd create distance and then resent them for not closing it. I'd been doing it my whole life and the betrayal in my marriage had turned the volume up to eleven. Knowing the pattern didn't make it disappear. But it meant I could catch myself in it and choose differently. That was the difference between my first relationship after divorce ~ which was a disaster ~ and my second one, which is actually good."*

Before You Swipe ~ The Inner Work First

There is a sequence that matters here, and it is one that the excitement of new possibility makes easy to skip. Do not skip it.

Know your non-negotiables. These are the things that are not negotiable ~ the values, the life circumstances, the relational qualities that are so fundamental to who you are and what you need that their absence is not something you can accommodate or grow past. They are different from preferences. Preferences are things you'd like but can compromise on. Non-negotiables are the ones where compromise means losing yourself.

Your non-negotiables might include: someone who is emotionally available and capable of genuine intimacy. Someone who is honest ~ not perfectly, but fundamentally and consistently. Someone whose vision for their life is compatible with yours in the ways that matter ~ about family, about geography, about how time and money are spent. Someone who treats people ~ all people, not just you ~ with basic kindness and respect. Someone who, when conflict arises, engages rather than disappears.

Know your dealbreakers too ~ the behaviors and patterns that, based on your history and your self-knowledge, you now recognize as incompatible with your well-being. These may be specific to your experience. If your marriage involved financial control, someone who is evasive about money may be a dealbreaker. If your marriage involved emotional unavailability, someone who dismisses your feelings early in dating may be a dealbreaker. These are not character judgments of other people. They are self-knowledge about what you cannot healthily sustain.

And know what you are actually looking for ~ at this particular moment in your life. Are you looking for deep partnership? For companionship without commitment? For the experience of dating as a form of self-discovery? For something casual that lets you practice being with new people without the weight of long-term stakes? All of these are valid. None of them are valid if you're not honest about them ~ with yourself first, and then with the people you date.

Be honest about where you are. Someone who is three months out of a marriage and not yet done grieving owes the people they date the truth of that ~ not as a disclosure dump on a first date, but as an honest orientation toward what they can genuinely offer right now. The person who pretends they are further along than they are, who performs readiness they don't feel, who pulls someone in and then has to pull back because the grief caught up with them ~ that costs both people something. Do the inner work first. Date from honest ground.

Building Confidence ~ Showing Up as Who You Are Now

Here is something almost everyone feels when they re-enter dating after a long marriage: a version of terror.

The dating landscape has changed. The rules feel different. Your body is different than it was when you last dated. Your life is more complicated ~ there may be children, there is certainly history, there are financial realities and time constraints and emotional textures that did not exist the last time you were doing this. And somewhere underneath all of it is the quiet, devastating voice that asks: am I still someone worth choosing?

Let me answer that directly: yes. You are. Not despite everything you have been through, but in some real way because of it. You are more self-aware than you were. You know more about what you need and what you cannot sustain. You have survived something genuinely hard and you are still standing and still reaching toward connection. That is not a liability. That is character.

Confidence in dating is not the absence of vulnerability. It is not performing certainty you don't feel or projecting a version of yourself that is more polished and less complicated than the truth. Real confidence in dating is the willingness to show up as who you actually are ~ imperfect, in-process, real ~ and to trust that the right person will find that person worth knowing.

Work on the things within your control. Take care of your body ~ not to make yourself acceptable to someone else, but because physical self-care is an act of respect toward yourself that radiates outward. Invest in your appearance in ways that make you feel like yourself. Pursue the interests and goals that make you interesting to yourself first. Because genuine engagement with your own life ~ the curiosity, the growth, the investment in becoming ~ is the most magnetic quality a person can have. It is infinitely more attractive than any performance of desirability.

Practice being in the world. Conversation is a skill. Flirtation is a skill. Presence ~ the ability to be genuinely interested in and interesting to another person in real time ~ is a skill. These skills get rusty during long marriages where the patterns of interaction are deeply familiar. Practice them in low-stakes settings. With the person next to you on a plane. With a new acquaintance at a community event. With anyone who invites conversation. Get comfortable being curious about strangers again. It is one of the best preparations for dating that exists.

Marcus: *"The first time I went on an actual date after my divorce I was forty-one years old and sweating like it was* *my first day of high school. I'd been with one person for over a decade. I had no idea what I was doing. I talked too much about my divorce. I asked weird questions. I knocked over my water glass. It was genuinely terrible. And then I went home and I laughed about it, and I realized that being terrible at something at the beginning is just being a beginner. I got better. You get better. You just have to survive the beginning first."*

Navigating the Modern Dating Landscape ~ Apps, Culture, and Protecting Your Heart

The dating landscape for someone re-entering after a long marriage can feel genuinely alien. The apps, the culture, the pace, the language ~ all of it has evolved, and if you've been partnered for a decade or more, you are walking into a world that changed significantly while you were away.

Dating apps are now the dominant way that adults meet romantic partners, particularly for LGBTQ+ people for whom the pool of potential partners in any given physical space may be limited. They are a tool ~ imperfect, gamified, occasionally dehumanizing, and also genuinely how real relationships begin every single day. Approach them as a tool rather than an oracle. They can introduce you to people you would never have encountered otherwise. They cannot tell you whether those people are right for you. That requires actual human interaction and the irreducible complexity of real connection.

For LGBTQ+ daters, the app landscape includes platforms specifically designed for your community ~ Grindr, Scruff, HER, Lex, Feeld, OkCupid with its extensive identity options, and others depending on your specific identity and what you're looking for. General apps like Hinge, Bumble, and Tinder have expanded their gender and orientation options significantly. Know which platforms serve your community and your specific intentions best, and know that the culture and norms differ significantly between apps. A little research before you dive in saves a lot of confusion.

Create a profile that is honest and specific. Generic profiles ~ the ones that say you love to laugh and enjoy good food and are looking for someone to go on adventures with ~ are invisible. Specific profiles are memorable. What actually makes you interesting? What are you genuinely passionate about? What kind of person are you actually looking for, described in concrete rather than aspirational terms? Honesty and specificity attract compatible people and repel incompatible ones, which is exactly what you want a profile to do.

Manage the pace. Dating apps have a way of creating a sense of urgency and volume that is at odds with how real connection actually develops. You do not need to match with everyone. You do not need to respond to every message within minutes. You do not need to move from matching to meeting in forty-eight hours because the app culture suggests that is the norm. Take the pace that feels right to you. Someone worth knowing will still be there if you take a day to respond.

Hookup culture and casual connection deserve a direct conversation ~ with yourself. The post-divorce period is, for many people, a time of sexual rediscovery. The end of a long marriage may have been preceded by years of a diminished or absent sexual relationship. The desire to reconnect with yourself as a sexual being ~ to feel desired, to feel alive in your body, to explore what you actually want now that you're not in the context of a specific partnership ~ is real and valid and entirely human.

Navigate this honestly. Know what you're looking for in any given connection and be honest about it with your potential partners. Casual connection pursued with honesty and mutual consent is very different from casual connection pursued through misleading someone about your intentions. The former is a legitimate way to meet your own needs. The latter creates harm and, often, additional grief that you do not need right now.

Safety reminder: Meet first dates in public places. Tell a trusted friend where you are going and who you are meeting.

Use your own transportation. Trust your instincts ~ if something feels off, it is okay to leave. These are not paranoid precautions. They are basic dignified self-care.

Setting Boundaries ~ And Actually Holding Them

Boundaries are one of those words that have become so prevalent in the wellness conversation that they've started to lose their meaning. So let me say what I actually mean.

A boundary is not a wall. It is not a punishment. It is not something you set to control another person's behavior. A boundary is a statement about what you will and will not participate in ~ a declaration of what is acceptable to you and what is not, followed by a consequence you are actually prepared to enforce if the line is crossed.

The second part of that definition is the part most people skip. A boundary without a consequence is a wish. If you tell someone that you need to be communicated with respectfully and when they communicate disrespectfully you say nothing and stay anyway, you have not set a boundary. You have expressed a preference and then demonstrated that it doesn't actually apply. This is confusing for the other person and corrosive for you.

Knowing your boundaries requires knowing yourself ~ which is why the identity work of Chapter 7 comes before the dating chapter. What are you not willing to tolerate in a relationship? What behaviors, when you encounter them in someone new, tell you that this is not a person you can safely open to? What do you need ~ in terms of communication, in terms of pace, in terms of physical and emotional respect ~ to feel safe enough to be real with someone?

Common post-divorce boundary territory: the pace of commitment. After a marriage ends, some people need to move slowly in new relationships to ensure they are genuinely choosing rather than defaulting. If someone is pushing for more commitment faster than you are ready for, that is information ~ both about their needs and about the compatibility of your timelines. You are allowed to name your pace and hold to it.

Introduction to your children. If you have children, when and how a new partner meets them is one of the most important decisions of the post-divorce dating period. There is no universal timeline. What is universally true is that children should not be introduced to someone new until you have a genuine sense of who that person is and where the relationship is going. They are not props in your dating life. They are vulnerable people who will form attachments to the people you bring into their world. Protect them.

Your past. You are allowed to share your history at the pace that feels right to you. You are not obligated to give a full accounting of your marriage and divorce on a first date, or a third date, or ever in more detail than you choose. Be honest ~ do not misrepresent your history or your current circumstances ~ but you control the depth and the timing of your own story.

Your emotional availability. If you are having a hard week ~ if the grief has surged unexpectedly, if a legal development has knocked you sideways, if you are simply depleted and do not have much to offer ~ you are allowed to say so. A partner worth having will receive that honestly and respond with care. A partner who cannot tolerate your humanness is telling you something important about whether they can truly show up for you.

Building Healthy Relationships ~ What They Actually Look Like

After a marriage that ended, your baseline for what a relationship feels like may need recalibration. If the marriage was high-conflict, you may have normalized tension that was not normal. If it was emotionally distant, you may have normalized disconnection that was not inevitable. If it involved any form of control or abuse, you may have normalized dynamics that were genuinely harmful and that will feel alarmingly familiar if they appear again in a new relationship ~ familiar enough that you might mistake the familiarity for comfort.

Healthy relationships do not feel like constant work. This is one of the most important recalibrations to make. Every relationship requires effort ~ communication, compromise, presence, continued investment. But there is a difference between the effort of two people actively building something together and the effort of one person constantly managing, appeasing, or recovering from the other. The former is what healthy partnership feels like. The latter is what exhaustion wears as a relationship.

Healthy relationships have conflict ~ and resolve it. The absence of conflict is not a sign of a healthy relationship. It is often a sign that someone is suppressing, accommodating, or disconnecting. Healthy couples fight ~ about real things, with real feelings ~ and then work through it. What distinguishes healthy conflict from unhealthy conflict is not the intensity but the conduct. Name-calling, contempt, stonewalling, and belittling are the markers of corrosive conflict. Honest disagreement, active listening, the willingness to be wrong and to repair ~ these are the markers of conflict that strengthens a relationship rather than eroding it.

Healthy relationships feel safe. This is the simplest and most essential marker. Do you feel safe being honest with this person? Safe being imperfect? Safe expressing a need or a boundary without bracing for punishment? Safe being wrong, being vulnerable, being in a hard season? Safety in a relationship is not the absence of challenge. It is the presence of trust ~ the bone-deep knowledge that this person is fundamentally for you, even when things are hard.

Healthy relationships support your individual wholeness. The right person does not require you to shrink. They do not ask you to give up the friendships, the interests, the ambitions, the pieces of your identity that belong to you rather than to the relationship. They celebrate those things. They are curious about them. They have their own equivalent wholeness ~ their own life, their own interests, their own sense of self that exists alongside the relationship rather than being subsumed by it. Two whole people building something together is categorically different from two people disappearing into each other.

Deja: *"I knew it was different with her when I disagreed with her about something ~ I don't even remember what ~ and she didn't shut down or get defensive. She said, 'Tell me more about why you see it that way.' I almost cried. Not because it was a grand gesture. Because it was so small and so normal and I realized I hadn't experienced that kind of basic curiosity about my perspective in years. That's when I understood how low my bar had gotten. And that's when I started raising it."*

A Word on Loving Again ~ The Risk Worth Taking

I want to close this chapter by speaking directly to the fear underneath all of it. Because beneath the practical questions about apps and timelines and boundaries and readiness, there is a quieter, more fundamental question that the experience of divorce plants in you:

What if I do this again and it ends again?

That is a reasonable fear. You loved someone ~ deeply, seriously, with the full intention of forever ~ and it didn't last. The thing you built your life around came apart. That experience leaves a mark. It makes the risk of love feel different than it did before. More weighted. More exposing. More genuinely dangerous.

I cannot promise you that the next relationship will last. I cannot promise you that love, entered into carefully and honestly and with everything you've learned, is guaranteed to work out. The only honest thing I can tell you is that love is always a risk. It was a risk the first time. It is a risk now. The difference is that you are not the same person you were the first time. You know more. You are clearer. You are less willing to tolerate what does not serve you and more capable of recognizing what does.

The goal is not to guarantee an outcome. The goal is to love from a place of wholeness rather than need. To choose someone from a place of genuine desire rather than fear of being alone. To build something new with eyes open and values clear and the hard-won self-knowledge of someone who has already been through the fire and walked out the other side.

That kind of love ~ conscious, chosen, clear-eyed ~ is not a diminished version of what you had before. It is a more evolved one. And it is available to you. When you are ready. On your timeline. Without apology.

"The most important thing in the world is to learn to give out love, and to let it come in." ~ Morrie Schwartz

You survived the ending of love. You are going to be extraordinary at the beginning of it.

The storm did not ask your permission.
Neither did the morning.

But here you are ~
standing in it.
Quiet.
Still here.

You are not who you were
when this began.

Good.
Let the grief be what it was.
Let the love be what it was.
Let all of it
have meant something.
Because it did.

There will be mornings
that ask nothing of you
but to exist in them.
Those mornings are coming.
Some of them are already here.

You survived the ending.
Now live the rest.

~ ***JC***

About the Author

J. Chester is the author of the Whispers in the Wind series and the novel The Wolf in the Gallery.

Writing across genres, J. Chester explores the interior life ~ instinct, resilience, the quiet work of healing, and the long journey back to trusting yourself.

~ Take Care

www.ingramcontent.com/pod-product-compliance
Lightning Source LLC
LaVergne TN
LVHW052306100826
845147LV00006B/686
* 9 7 9 8 9 8 8 4 6 4 8 2 2 *